MARCH HARES
AND
MONKEYS' UNCLES

MARCH HARES
AND
MONKEYS' UNCLES

BY

HARRY OLIVER

metro

Published by Metro Publishing
an imprint of John Blake Publishing Ltd
3 Bramber Court, 2 Bramber Road,
London W14 9PB, England

www.johnblakepublishing.co.uk

First published in paperback in 2008

ISBN: 978 1 84454 670 1

British Library Cataloguing-in-Publication Data:

A catalogue record for this book is available from the British Library.

Design by www.envydesign.co.uk

Printed and bound by ⚒ Grafica Veneta S.p.A., Trebaseleghe (PD) - Italy

5 7 9 10 8 6 4

© Text copyright Harry Oliver, 2008

Papers used by John Blake Publishing are natural, recyclable products
made from wood grown in sustainable forests. The manufacturing processes
conform to the environmental regulations of the country of origin.

Every attempt has been made to contact the relevant copyright-holders,
but some were unobtainable. We would be grateful if the appropriate
people could contact us.

For James, who certainly had a way with words.

This book is dedicated to the memory of
James Ravenscroft, my dear friend and
co-author, who died tragically and suddenly
a week after the completion of this book.
His enlivening, endlessly funny company turned
what could have been painstaking hours of
research and writing into a wonderful roller-
coaster ride of laughter, arguments and ideas.
Working together was sometimes a distraction,
and a tea break would often turn into an
afternoon of pretending to be penning 'the book'
while really just having a chinwag. But we got
there. Without him none of this would have
happened, and I will never forget him for the
loveable, superb character that he was.

ALSO BY HARRY OLIVER

Black Cats and April Fools
Origins of the old wives'
tales and superstitions in
our daily lives

Cat Flaps and Mousetraps
The origins of objects in
our daily lives

Bees' Knees and Barmy Armies
The much-awaited
follow-up to *March Hares
and Monkeys' Uncles*

Available in all good bookshops, priced £9.99.
To order a copy directly visit blake.co.uk

CONTENTS

ACKNOWLEDGEMENTS

There are so many to thank that the order in which I do so is somewhat arbitrary. But the first person has to be Sarah Marshall, James's fiancée, who endured many an evening and weekend of James and me covering their home with paper and typing away. Where would we have been without those sturdy, nutritious veggie dinners and your patient encouragement?

Heartfelt thanks for the huge amount of ideas and suggestions from friends and family. Particular thanks are due to Mandy Kirby for excellent research links, Gill Partington and Eleanor Chiari for their sound academic advice and Nicki Malliaros for fascinating entry suggestions.

I am very grateful to Mike Mosedale for his wonderful illustrations. Always a pleasure to work with, your patience and humility when asked to make changes to drafts (which of course meant redrawing entire pictures) was truly admirable! Your attention to detail and humour is much appreciated. Many thanks also to Graeme Andrew, for the brilliant cover design. Judging this book by its cover, it's a corker.

My editor Adam Parfitt worked his magic with characteristic style, picking out the contradictions and shortcomings of the text with enviable efficiency. I can't thank you enough, Ad.

INTRODUCTION

In spite of the fact that we continually use hundreds of words and phrases to communicate with one another, we rarely take the time to consider why they mean what they do, or where they come from. After all, most of us have better things to do – at least we should have! To do much more than briefly ponder the sense in 'turning over a new leaf' when we vow to change our ways is simply not something most of us have time for. But think about it and you might start to wonder: what exactly is a new leaf, and why would anyone turn it over, and what has this got to do with starting again? There is nearly always an answer, but it is not always easy to find.

Indeed, if one were to attempt to get to the bottom of the origins of just a few choice expressions from our endlessly rich language, one's 'work would be cut out' to the point that the most likely result would be nothing more than a stonking headache – but why 'stonking'? The point is that we take our language for granted as a matter of necessity. I feel very lucky about this, for it means there's a whole cosmos of intrigue, history and humour lying behind the words we bandy around that I am sure will captivate anyone who utters words in English today.

I set out to achieve three things when writing this book. To inform, to entertain, and to avoid making people yawn. Within its pages are a substantial number of widely used phrases, and a cluster of less well-known and quirky ones that will be welcome additions to anyone's vocabulary – it is hoped that all of them will provide memorable and diverting answers to the questions that may be posed about their origins. This is by no means a comprehensive guide to the history of English, but a fun volume that maintains historical accuracy when explaining some truly interesting parts of our everyday speech.

Often, when trying to find the origin of a

choice word or phrase, it was hard not to 'come a cropper' as a result of diverse opinions about its true background. But instead of 'throwing in the towel', I decided to either give the definition with the most credible and popular explanation or, where it was too close to call, I have simply given the possibilities and left the reader to ponder the somewhat imponderable.

If there's not something in here for everyone I'll 'eat my hat', even though I don't own one, and if there's anyone out there who enjoys a bit of 'nit-picking' and would like to make any suggestions or corrections for improvements in subsequent editions, or if you simply have an 'axe to grind', then please 'keep your pants on' and email my publisher: words@blake.co.uk. I'm sure if there are any linguistic differences between us we can find a way to 'bury the hatchet'.

Thank you for dipping into your wallets to buy this book – although I do hope you didn't acquire it on the 'black market'. Either way I would be most pleased if you enjoy its pages enough conclude that it would be 'cheap at half the price'. Happy reading!

CHAPTER ONE:
FOOD AND DRINK

Spitting Feathers

FOOD AND DRINK

Biscuit
Comes from the Latin *panis biscoctus* meaning 'bread baked twice', via the Old French *bescuit*. The second baking of dough dried it out, creating the crispy texture that's so familiar, as well as encouraging it to keep well.

Butter wouldn't melt in his mouth
This phrase has been in use since at least the fifteenth century, but its origins are pretty much unknown. We use it when speaking of a person whose exterior meekness and gentility belies the true awfulness of their nature, which

is the opposite of innocent! What is interesting about the phrase is that, when examined, we might have some trouble making sense of the metaphor. After all, if taken literally it is quite absurd – whether they are good or bad, butter *will* always melt in someone's mouth. Perhaps the phrase, which is at least 500 years old, developed out of a sense of someone being so cool, calm and collected that, figuratively speaking, even one of the most easily melted substances would remain unchanged when brought into contact with them. Such a person would surely be a pretty sinister fellow, capable of still more sinister acts of deception!

Caesar salad

The salad is named after Caesar Gardini, the owner–chef at a restaurant called Caesar's Place in Tijuana, Mexico. The Italian chef invented the dish in 1924 over the 4 July weekend. Legend has it that the kitchen had pretty much run out of food and he constructed the salad from what was left: romaine lettuce, garlic, olive oil, croutons, eggs and parmesan cheese.

4

Cheesy

The moment when we hear or see something that is truly cheesy is not a pleasant one. It might be a lyric on the radio that is so gooey and silly it makes us physically ill, or a plot line in a film that is so contrived and contains such unrestricted sentimentality you can do nothing but feel grimly cynical. The word 'cheesy' describes the similarly stifling effect of overripe cheese on its victim.

Cold shoulder

To give someone the cold shoulder is to blank them and make them feel uncomfortable. Tradition has it that, when a guest of a large household had outstayed their welcome, the host would serve them a meal of cold meat, usually a shoulder of mutton, to indicate that it was time they left. This is an unlikely explanation, not least because cold meat is often tasty, so if the guest was a glutton – and if they had overstayed their welcome, why wouldn't they be? – they might not get the message. The earliest reference to this phrase seems to be from the novel *The Antiquary* by Sir Walter

Scott, which was published in 1816: 'The Countess's dislike didna gang farther at first than just showing o' the cauld shouther.' The phrase is born solely from the writer's inventive use of language in describing an elaborate variation of the age-old snub of turning one's back on someone.

Cut the mustard

Exactly how cutting the mustard came to mean an expression of being able to perform well and with flare cannot be precisely determined. What is pretty sure is that mustard became synonymous with all that was good around the late nineteenth and early twentieth century, when the mustard paste that is familiar to us all became commercially popular. If something was 'the proper mustard', it was excellent and how it should be. There are suggestions that cutting the mustard refers to harvesting the plant, which is difficult to grow, so someone who could not cut the mustard would not be able to produce the real thing.

Foot the bill

The phrase appears in the fifteenth century, when it meant nothing more than adding up the various components of the bill and writing them at the bill's foot. Over time, however, it has come to mean pay the bill rather than add it up.

Hill of beans

The phrase hill of beans, the origins of which are American, was popularised in Humphrey Bogart's immortal closing words in *Casablanca*. Speaking to Ingrid Bergman, Bogie observes that 'it doesn't take much to see that the problems of three people don't amount to a hill of beans in this crazy world' – unforgettable stuff, but why hill of beans? The phrase dates from the mid-nineteenth century when it was used, unsurprisingly, in the world of bean-growing. In this case, an actual hill of beans was being referred to, but over time the phrase was adopted as a figurative expression of worthlessness – the seemingly faulty logic behind this being that, if one bean had no value, nor would a great mound of them. It is a peculiar phrase that, when examined, makes little metaphorical sense.

In the soup

Used to state that someone is in trouble or in an unfavourable position, this phrase dates from Ireland's potato famine during the 1840s. When the famine was at its peak, many of Dublin's population depended on soup kitchens for sustenance. However, to receive soup, Irish families had to renounce Catholicism, convert to Protestantism and anglicise their names. O'Connor became Connor, O'Donohue became Donohue, and so on. This was a degrading and painful sacrifice, but many were forced to comply because they were in such dire need of adequate nutrition. Thus, to be in the soup was to be in trouble and in need.

Jerusalem artichoke

Not only are Jerusalem artichokes not artichokes, but they are also not from Jerusalem. The plant itself resembles a sunflower and it has edible tuberous roots. They were named *girasole* by the Italians, which means sun-circler (like sunflowers, the flower heads turn to face the sun as it passes over during the day). Sloppy pronunciation of *girasole* came to sound like something resembling Jerusalem. They were originally named artichokes because they were thought to taste similar to globe artichokes.

Make no bones about it

To make no bones about a subject is to discuss it very frankly, or to make a statement about a delicate matter without hesitation or thought for the feelings of others. Nowadays always associated with straight talking, the phrase has culinary origins. It grew out of the fourteenth-century phrase to find bones in something, a figurative expression meaning to have a problem with or be opposed to an idea or action. It found its literal origin in any food where unwanted bones could present themselves as unexpected obstacles to happy eating. The opposite of finding bones was, unsurprisingly, to find no bones, which of course meant to have no objections, to be satisfied. It can easily be seen how finding no bones engendered making no bones, the latter

9

taking on an extra sense of deliberate creation of complications or objections.

Mullered
A slang word that means destructively inebriated on drugs or drink. It most likely derives from the word mulled, which has a close connection with alcoholic drink – as in mulled wine.

One over the eight
The fact that this phrase is practically unknown in the US but is used in the UK and Ireland speaks volumes about the difference in how alcohol is viewed on either side of the Atlantic. To be one over the eight is to be drunk. It doesn't mean horribly drunk, just a bit too drunk. The logic behind the expression is that, while eight beers are within bounds of something approaching reasonable sobriety, nine beers is a beer too far. It is not clear if there is any degree of irony involved in the expression. There certainly ought to be.

Peach Melba
The Australian opera singer Nellie Melba was

christened Helen Mitchell, but she gave herself the stage name of Melba in tribute to the city of Melbourne. She became the darling of the Covent Garden Opera House during the late 1800s. The renowned French chef Auguste Escoffier was a great fan and, in tribute to her performance of Elsa in Wagner's *Lohengrin*, he replicated the swan from the first act in ice. Between the wings of the swan he served the dish, which consisted of poached peaches on a bed of vanilla ice cream. Later he added raspberry purée to the ensemble and the Peach Melba was born.

Proof's in the pudding

A more popular abbreviation of 'The proof of the pudding is in the eating' – a caution to all who are blinded by razzle-dazzle. While something may look good, appearances can cover a multitude of sins.

Save one's bacon

To save your bacon is to prevent an injury or loss to yourself, often by a narrow margin, and sometimes at the expense of someone else's misfortune. The phrase arose as a metaphor from the necessity of keeping the household's winter store of bacon protected from scavenging dogs. In this sense its meaning is to prevent a loss. The phrase became more established between the eleventh and nineteenth centuries, when a number of expressions used bacon and other pig-related terms as metaphors for people, mainly because in the mid- to late Middle Ages bacon was for ordinary country folk the only affordable meat. This led to words like pig, swine and hog being used by aristocrats when describing the less well-off. For example, Norman lords referred to Saxons as hogs, and a chaw-bacon was an unpleasant term for a farm worker, chaw meaning chew. It is interesting that today the use of the phrase often carries overtones of slightly swine-like, selfish behaviour.

Shambles

If something is a bit of a shambles it is untidy and chaotic. A teenager's room, for example, is likely to be a constant shambles and, when instructed to do so by an exasperated parent, the youngster's attempts to rectify the mess will often be shambolic. The word derives from *scamel*, a Saxon word meaning a stall displaying meat. In towns up and down Britain, the Shambles was traditionally a street containing butchers' shops and markets. By the end of the working day, the street was often littered with the remnants of unwanted meat, wrappings and the general by-products of quite a messy trade, and so the name became synonymous with any sort of undesirable mess.

Sow one's wild oats

The phrase sow one's wild oats is nearly always used in a sexual context, and usually to convey a sense of abandonment and irresponsibility. There is a rather obvious connection between a man's sexual function and the sowing of seeds, but the origin of this euphemism is particularly interesting. Unsurprisingly perhaps, it is in farming. Centuries ago, farmers were plagued by the existence of wild oats, a type of grass that grew throughout Europe (as it does today). It is unusable as a crop, and is also frustratingly hard to separate from useful cereal. The only way to do so used to be by handpicking them in the fields. They always grew back though, so the whole process was endlessly frustrating. Therefore, to sow wild oats would be an utterly useless activity, and the idea of this became a metaphor for people, especially men, who used their time unwisely. The more recent association with sex came about because of the comparison of seeds with sperm, and in this sense being promiscuous can, in crass terms, lead to an unwanted crop.

Spitting feathers

We commonly use this phrase to describe someone in a state of very obvious anger or distress, someone who looks so incensed that they may really lose control. Yet the original (some might say 'proper') meaning of the term was somewhat different – it meant to be thirsty. To have a mouthful of feathers would, we can all assume, be a pretty unpleasant experience. We can easily see that spitting feathers was used figuratively to indicate a dry, unpleasant palette in need of a good watering, or perhaps a good old cup of tea. It cannot be denied that the need for a drink can lead to a degree of irritation in a person, but rarely does fancying a pint lead to spitting feathers in the sense of displaying outrage! So how did it come to refer to such behaviour? The only answer is that, at some point in the 1960s, the phrase was adopted and given a new meaning. It is highly likely that, because of its similarity to the phrase spitting blood – which has always meant to be angry – spitting feathers was seized upon by a number of persons who didn't know any better (or perhaps were simply never thirsty!) and used as a softer substitute for the grimmer image.

Storm in a teacup

This is a phrase used to describe a fuss having been made over nothing of any real consequence, or when an argument has erupted over a trifling matter. If we read the phrase literally, the idea of a storm taking place in such a tiny, localised space suggests not only an event of insignificance, but also a sense of absurdity – a literal storm in a teacup is impossible, yet figuratively it works, especially because we often use the phrase in retrospect, having realised that the fuss was as ridiculous as a storm in a teacup. It was unnecessary and should not have happened, yet, figuratively speaking, it somehow managed to. There are other examples of similar phrases in the *Oxford English Dictionary*, such as storm in a cream bowl and storm in a wash-hand basin.

Tab

Most commonly a word for credit given by publicans to trusted, regular customers, a bar tab was originally a slate on which money owed for drinks was chalked up until the customer was able to pay his debt, when the slate would literally be wiped clean. Tab is short for 'tablet', which is in turn another word for a writing slate. The person responsible for monitoring the loans was the tally man. Often, small, individual tabs were produced for each borrower – the tally man and the customer would each have a marked-up slate as a way of ensuring that the amounts 'tallied' and nobody was conned.

Take the piss

This modern phrase is the vulgar cousin of take

the mickey, yet is much easier to understand. It stems from the obscure phrase piss-proud, a term describing the state of a gentleman who, on awakening, discovers he has an erection. A man whose sexual function has been, shall we say, letting him down might be rather pleased and proud to discover himself in such a state of excitement. On realising that his state is not owing to a new lease of virility but, rather, to his need to urinate, he may be rather dismayed and realise that he has been deceiving himself. It is easy to see how this works as a metaphor. To take the piss out of someone, then, is to remind them of their delusions in a way that can be embarrassing and funny. A second sense of the phrase, meaning to talk nonsense or behave strangely and inappropriately, finds its explanation in a memorable historical anecdote. The story goes that Ancient Siberian shamans were very fond of the red and white *Amanita muscaria* mushroom (also known as the fly agaric), a sacred fungus containing potent hallucinogenic compounds that were an aid to their rituals. The human body, however, cannot tolerate the poisons that are also present in this mushroom. The shamans got around this by feeding large quantities of it to their reindeer (who also seemed to enjoy its effects). Once it had passed through the creatures' bodies, the urine-soaked snow would be 'taken' and eaten by the Shamans who, becoming high on the drug, would proceed to talk less sense than before. It was easy to spot someone who had literally taken the piss, or was in the process of taking it.

Teetotal

A common belief is that this word refers to someone who has given up alcohol and chosen tea as their alternative tipple. But this pleasingly neat explanation falls down when attention is drawn to the incorrectly spelled tee. To accept this definition would be to overlook the fact that tee has never been an alternative spelling of tea. The true story behind the word is more diverting. It was born in a speech by an Englishman, Richard 'Dicky' Turner. Somewhat ironically, Dicky was a reformed alcoholic whose devotion to temperance leaned towards the extreme. For him, the only way to abstain was to deny oneself all forms of booze, be it beer, wine or spirits. One day, while speaking on the subject, and demanding total abstinence, he stuttered on the word 't-t-total' and, since he was a such an extreme advocate of temperance, the mistake was seized upon by the congregation and became the word to define an abstainer.

Through the mill
When wheat or corn was ground in the traditional way, it was done so by placing two enormous and very heavy circular stones on top of each other. The cereal was then fed into a hole in the top stone and the top stone was rotated. This action propelled the cereal between the gaps in the stone out towards the edge. By the time the seeds reached the edge of the stones they were ground to a fine powder – flour. To be put through the mill is to survive a similarly arduous process in life.

Toast
At weddings we toast the bride and groom; at funerals we may even toast the departed – but why 'toast'? The word has an odd history. In the

twelfth century the quality of the wine and ale on offer was nowhere near as palatable as what we today consider to be a good tipple, and it was common practice to dip spiced toast into alcoholic beverages to draw bad flavours from it. How exactly this worked is a bit of a mystery, but it happened nonetheless and the tradition carried on for centuries until the quality of the booze improved. In the 1600s, the practice of raising a toast to a special member of a party emerged. The idea was that the guest became a figurative piece of toast that improved the flavour of the wine – a form of flattery that continues to this day, where we toast not only people but also events, concepts and, of course, good health.

Wet one's whistle

To wet your whistle is to take a drink in order to hydrate a dry mouth. The likening of the mouth and throat to a whistle comes from the fact that it is very hard to whistle a tune with a dry mouth. Simple.

You can't teach your grandmother to suck eggs

The phrase is applied when a young person is

trying to tell an older, and therefore presumably more experienced, person a hard fact of life. It has a rather distasteful origin. In the not-too-distant past, dental hygiene was not what it is today. With age, a person's teeth fell out. Dentures were expensive and often unreliable. One of the few foods available to the standard toothless grandmother would have been a hard-boiled, or possibly pickled, egg, which she could suck down with ease. Instructing your grandmother how to suck down eggs would have been as tactless as it would have been pointless.

CHAPTER TWO:
NAMES

Happy As Larry

NAMES

Boycott

A word that means to abandon dealings with a person or organisation, or to refuse to buy a product, usually as a means of protest. It is a commonly used word born out of a moment in nineteenth-century Irish history. It is based on one Captain Charles Cunningham Boycott, an Englishman who was serving as an estate agent on the farming properties of Lord Earne in the late nineteenth century during a period of upheaval in the landholding system. He was a deeply disliked man, and campaigns organised by the Irish Land League, led by Charles Stuart

Parnell, sought to force Boycott to heavily discount their rents. But Boycott was a stubborn character, and was having none of it. Parnell decided that there was only one way to persuade him to reconsider: refuse to deal with him! Amazingly, everyone in the region agreed with Parnell and began to treat him like 'the lepers of old'. Soon enough, Boycott could not get anyone to do anything for him – shops would not sell to him, and his workmen quit. Any help he got came from those drafted in from elsewhere in the country. Boycott stood firm, but rapidly the practice became known as boycotting, and a new verb was born. His name became an instant word for mass abandonment – before life boycotted Boycott, he saw his name enter into the language as a standard term.

Freudian slip
A slip of the tongue that results in an errant word, which may have something humorous to say about the speaker. If someone were to look up in a noisy office and declare 'I can't drink!' instead of 'I can't think!' it would be a classic

26

Freudian slip. The term, of course, derives from Freud's belief that the subconscious can manifest itself in one's behaviour.

Gordon Bennett

Astonishingly there really was a Gordon Bennett. Incredibly perhaps, there were two. The first, James Gordon Bennett, was a Scotsman who established the *New York Herald* for $500 in 1835. In less than a year, the circulation had climbed to 15,000 copies every day. He developed many innovations that we now take for granted in newspapers, such as illustrations to go with the news columns and the use of telecommunications in the form of the nineteenth-century telegraph network. His son (James Gordon Bennett II) went into the family business and, true to the archetype of a fabulously wealthy man, went about his life with serious *joie de vivre*. He took over the running of the *Herald* in 1867. Among his notable achievements was financing a journalist named Henry Stanley on a trip to Africa to find the missing British explorer Dr Livingstone. After this and many other international scoops,

Bennett Jr decamped to Paris where he became legendary for his sporting exploits, which included yachting and ballooning. His name was well known enough in the UK to stand in for the popular oath 'gorblimey!' (a truncated version of 'God blind me!'). Among discerning speakers, it remains an affectionate tribute to the surprising and improbable.

Gringo
An often derogatory term used by Mexicans for Americans. The original word was not applied exclusively to Americans, or to Spanish-speaking Mexicans; in fact it was used as far back as 1787 by Spanish speakers to describe foreigners whose command of Spanish was poor. In Madrid at that time, it tended to refer to the Irish. It is probably a corruption of the Spanish *greigo*, meaning Greek, and it conveys a similar sense as the English expression 'It's all Greek to me!'

Guillotine
It is sometimes thought that the Guillotine was named after Dr Joseph Ignace Guillotin because

he invented it. In fact, he didn't invent it. Similar machines purpose-built for beheading have been around in Europe since the 1100s. Dr Guillotin proposed using them because they were a 'humane' way of executing prisoners, better than hanging or being broken on the wheel. However, it was another doctor, Dr Antoine Louis, who actually designed the blueprint for the models used during the French Revolution, and for a time they were called 'louisons' or 'louisettes'. However, eventually they became know as guillotines. Guillotine himself was almost guillotined and his family didn't appreciate the association, so they changed their names. The efficiency of the guillotine as an execution device was impressive, and Belgium, Germany, Switzerland, Sweden and Vietnam as well as France used the machine well into the twentieth century.

Happy as Larry

To be as happy as Larry is, quite simply, to be perfectly pleased and satisfied with oneself and one's situation. But who is Larry, we may wonder. The phrase dates from the 1870s in

Australia, and the happy Larry is often said to have been one Larry Foley, a celebrated boxer who was instrumental in introducing gloves to the ring, thereby marginalising the bare-knuckled variety of the sport. It is assumed that his successes made him a happy man, and that the phrase sprang from this. If this explanation lacks punch on its own, it is strengthened when we observe the Aussie slang word larrikin, meaning a happy-go-lucky young tearaway who may cause a spot of bother here and there. A euphonic connection between Larry Foley and the word larrikin made the perfect basis for a jolly term.

Heath Robinson

A Heath Robinson affair or solution is a situation or turn of events characterised by complication and confusion. Heath Robinson was a cartoonist whose trademark drawing style was to illustrate pieces of equipment or apparatus that were intended to carry out elementary tasks, but to intentionally make their design complex. The result was elaborate and often humorously fantastical devices that served little purpose other than as entertaining cartoons. Had they been constructed, which would probably have been incredibly difficult to achieve, they would have been of no use as that which they were designed to achieve would always have been much easier to realise without the equipment. The phrase grew out of this sense of unnecessary and infuriatingly funny complication to be applied generally to situations outside of the cartoon world – or perhaps more accurately to situations that should be the stuff of cartoons – and is now more commonly applied to situations or things that appear quickly cobbled together and temporary, rather than well considered or useful.

Know your onions

To know your onions is to be an expert on a particular subject. Someone who has an encyclopaedic understanding of the biology of the onion and its place in social and natural history could be said to know his onions, but so too could an esteemed authority on nautical knots. The phrase can refer to any type of specialist, and it came about as the result of a particular specialist, one CT Onions, a venerated twentieth-century lexicographer and general word buff. His work on the *Oxford English Dictionary* led him to be so highly thought of that his name became a byword for his subject. A phrase was born and it caught on.

Mesmerism

Friedrich Anton Mesmer was a German physician who believed that hidden healing powers could be tapped. He named these forces 'animal magnetism'. By hypnotising his patients, he believed magnetic forces could be harnessed to cure their ailments. The medical authorities took a dim view of all this, and he was forced to leave Vienna. The word mesmerism was originally used to describe the medical application of hypnosis, although now it has come to pertain to anything that seems to have an uncanny hold of our attention.

Nicknames

I have two friends who illustrate a classic use of the nickname, both of whom are called John. The one from Wales is named Welsh John; the other rather taller John is named Long John. The addition of pertinent information before a proper name dates from times when surnames were not in use. These extra names were called *ekenames*. 'Eke', in this context, is Old English for 'addition'. Over time, the phrase 'an ekename' elided to form 'a nickname'.

Nosy parker

A nosy parker is someone only too content to take an interest in other people's business that is really no concern of his or hers. The idea of someone sticking their nose into private matters is a fun, figurative image that has come to work perfectly to sum up a certain type of annoyingly curious individual that we all find irritating. The original nosy parker was a sixteenth-century Archbishop of Canterbury, Matthew Parker, who served under Elizabeth I. He was a keen church reformer and was obsessed with delving into the lives of those answerable to him, much to the dismay of many in the Church. His reputation for prying and giving orders led to a phrase being coined – using one's 'nose' was figuratively an extreme (and comic) way for a

33

human to enquire into something, or to sniff something out, so 'nosy' became the perfect word to prefix Parker. The phrase has stuck through history.

Pommie

Australian slang for a British person. It is thought that this word is derived from an Australian form of cockney rhyming slang. Pomegranate was rhyming slang for immigrant, so a new British person arriving to the already colonised Australia was regarded as an immigrant by the white indigenous people. Pomegranate is then shortened to 'Pom' or 'Pommie'.

Surname

Some explanations of this word suggest that surname is a corruption of *sire*name. This implies that the name you get is passed on from the person by whom you were sired. However, surname hasn't been corrupted. The prefix 'sur–' actually means above – think of *sur*mount or *sur*pass. Your surname stands above your first name, indicating the general family to which you belong.

Take the mickey

If you are taking the mickey out of someone, or indeed having the mickey taken out of you, you are not only mocking them, but you are also engaging with a shortened version of a phrase derived from its ancestor 'to take the mickey bliss', which is cockney rhyming slang for taking the piss. The problem with understanding this expression lies in the choice of the name Mickey, short for Michael. Why Michael? For that matter, why bliss? At the end of the day it's hard to be sure, and anyone who tells you they know the truth about this phrase's beginnings is probably themselves extracting the Michael (a faux-polite variation on the phrase).

Tarmac

This word began life as the name of a Scotsman. John McAdam arrived back from America in the late 1700s having had a lucrative career in New York as an 'agent for prizes', which involved the redistribution of seized goods. On his return he began patching up his newly purchased estate which, among other things, involved repairing the roads. He used layers of small, tightly packed stones to create a smoother road surface. The process was a revelation, and a cheap one too. The technique was expanded on by Richard Edgeworth, who filled the gaps between the stones by mixing stone dust with water. This was called water macadam. Eventually the technique was adapted to combine tar with the stones to provide the most hardwearing surface of all. Tarmacadam was born. The shortened word tarmac was eventually patented, and, rather like Hoover and Xerox, the Tarmac company became so successful that their brand grew to be synonymous with road surfaces in general.

The George and Dragon

A celebration of the myth of St George, which appeared around the twelfth century. While travelling through Libya, St George is said to have slain a dragon who had been demanding the daily sacrifice of a young woman. The Libyans were down to the king's daughter. St George stepped in to save her by attacking the dragon under its wing where it had no scales to defend against his blade. In reality, it is thought that St George was born in Turkey in AD 270. He joined the Roman army, but protested against the emperor's persecution of his fellow Christians. He was thrown into jail and, despite being tortured, remained steadfast in his faith. He was eventually beheaded in Lydda in Palestine in AD 303. He is also a patron saint of Palestine and Portugal.

The Kings Arms
The common pub name the Kings Arms is a simple expression of allegiance to the king of the day.

The Nags Head
The Nags Head usually indicates that livery stables were once associated with the tavern. Livery stables were stables where horses could be hired or looked after. Originally the name would have provided a helpful aid to any traveller planning a long journey.

The White Hart
Hart is an archaic word for stag. Many pubs are so named because the white hart was the

emblem of Richard II, who ruled from 1377 to 1399. He chose the animal as his favoured symbol because it represents purity and mystery, and is rooted in English tradition. It also has mythical connections with Christianity, where the white stag came to symbolise Jesus Christ, and he felt its selection would convey his nobility and unequivocal right to rule as a divinely anointed monarch. Unfortunately for him, he was eventually deposed …

CHAPTER THREE:
MILITARY

Armed To The Teeth

MILITARY

Armed to the teeth
A popular explanation of this term is that it is a pirate phrase originating in Port Royal, Jamaica in the 1600s. Having only single-shot black-powder weapons and cutlasses, pirates would carry many of these weapons at once to keep up the fight. In addition they carried a knife in their teeth for maximum arms capability. But, contrary to most people's idea that warriors with knives and daggers form the basis of this phrase, it actually has little to do with such fearsome feats. To the teeth is a fourteenth-century phrase meaning fully and completely, rather like up to your neck.

AWOL

This acronym – for Absent Without Leave – was first used during the American Civil War. When deserters were caught, they were made to wear a placard bearing these initials. The reason why the O is included is to emphasise the fact that the soldier is absent with*out* leave, as opposed to AWL – Absent With Leave. It became pronounced as a word during the Second World War.

Blockbuster

We speak of a blockbuster in reference to hugely popular films, and sometimes to bestselling novels. The term suggests the notion of something being grandiose, incredible and awesome, and its modern meaning stems not from the world of entertainment, but that of war. The original blockbusters were bombs, used during the Second World War in air raids on Germany, that could destroy entire buildings in one explosion. We can quite clearly see how the term has been adopted – the 'block' that is busted now is the mind of the viewer or reader (block being slang for head), which is figuratively blown away by the power of the film or book.

Cockpit

Cockpits were the squalid areas up and down Britain in which cockfights took place before cockfighting was banned. During the First World War, pilots adopted this name for the unpleasant, cramped quarters from which they had to fly their planes.

D-Day

The D in D-Day is there to reinforce the 'Day' part of the phrase. However, D-Day has a technical function in a military context. It defines a day on which an operation begins, and allows an operation to be planned without having to mention dates. The following days are known as D+1, D+2, D+3 and so on. A less well-known variation is H-Hour, which works on the same principle. The D-Day that has become famous is 6 June 1944 when Allied forces landed in Normandy. In fact, it was intended to be on 5 June, but bad weather forced a delay. Because the operation was planned around a D-Day and not a fixed date, the plans did not have to be changed.

43

Drop the hammer

To drop the hammer on someone is to kill them. The hammer referred to in this case is the hammer of a gun, which is cocked before the shot is fired. When the gunman pulls the trigger, the hammer 'drops' and ignites the gun cartridge, which fires the bullet, which kills the person.

Flying by the seat of your pants

This is used to describe one's reactions and decisions when one strays into uncharted territory. The term dates back to the time when aeroplane pilots did not have the benefit of the many dials and buzzers familiar to the pilots of today. They had to rely on the immediate feedback they felt through the plane's fuselage, and the point of greatest contact with the plane could be found housed in the pilot's pants.

GI

This moniker for American soldiers is often thought to be satirical, the letters standing for 'government issue' or 'general issue', and the idea being that the soldier is a manufactured product of the government. In fact, GI once stood for 'galvanised iron', and this was stamped on the base of military-issue metal buckets.

Ground Zero

The former site of the World Trade Center in New York. The term originally describes the point closest to the impact of a blast, and was first used to refer to the effect of the two devastating atomic bombs that were dropped on Japan at the end of the Second World War. Newspaper reports described the effect the bomb had at distances away from 'ground zero', the epicentre of the bomb's impact.

Moaning Minnie

A moaning Minnie is someone who whines on unpleasantly and distracts everyone from getting on with what they want to be doing. However, it was coined to describe not people but the sound of an explosive trench mortar in the First World War called a *minenwerfer*. The *minenwerfer* made a loud whining sound as it flew through the air, and Minnie is an anglicised abbreviation of the German. The term was used during the Second World War to describe air-raid sirens, and in the eighties Mrs Thatcher used it to describe those who were critical of how many unemployed people there seemed to be under her administration.

Mole

A mole is a secret agent who operates in an enemy country without that country's knowledge of the agent being there. They may not actually do very much for long periods of time but, when the forces to which they are affiliated decide they need their mole, they are 'activated'. The word mole conveys the idea of an unseen burrower into a country's defences – you might not see it, but it's there anyway. The term was made popular by the fiction of John Le Carré, and is now actually used by intelligence agencies to describe such secret agents – a case of the real world borrowing from art.

Molotov cocktail

Vyacheslav Molotov was the Russian foreign minister during the Second World War. He personally had nothing to do with the creation of the Molotov cocktail. The phrase was used by the Finnish, who felt that Molotov was responsible for the Russian tanks that had rolled into their country during the winter of 1939–40. A bottle was filled with petrol and a rag stuffed in the top; the rag was lit and then the whole thing would be thrown at the offending tank, and the weapon was named after the hated foreign minister.

On a wing and a prayer

To be living, or to do something, on a wing and a prayer is to be in an extremely precarious situation where there is little one can do other than hope to come out of it safely; or to take a course of action that is necessary, yet still a huge risk. It is American in origin, and comes from a hit Second World War song, released in 1942, that describes a pilot returning to base from an successful air raid as 'comin' in on a wing and a prayer'. Flying 'on [one] wing' would have meant that one of the plane's engines had stopped, and quite obviously this is a very risky situation where luck or prayers might play a large part in returning the pilot to the ground.

47

Over the top

Excessive or foolhardy behaviour. In the First World War, to go over the top described a charge in trench warfare where soldiers would climb out of their trenches and go towards the enemy. The manoeuvre was notorious among infantrymen as survival against enemy machine guns was poor. The most infamous example of going over the top was the first day of the Battle of the Somme, 1 July 1916: 58,000 casualties were sustained by the British in that one day. A third of the casualties were fatal. This grim record still stands as the greatest number of casualties ever sustained by an army a single day.

Pass muster

To pass muster is to pass a test, whatever it may be. The expression is military in origin. To muster is to call together a group of troops for inspection. If the troops were correctly turned out, they would be described as having passed muster.

Stonking

A word used in a variety of instances to provide

emphasis. You might have a stonking tune, a stonking great car or even a stonking hangover. It seems most likely to have been appropriated from the old British military word 'stonk', which meant an intensive bombardment. It's easy to see how the word then became one that enforces others, but its popularity has no doubt spread because of its terrific sound.

Swashbuckling

Many of us will associate the word swash-buckling with pirates – the word conjures images of flamboyant fight scenes in adventure films, of swords clashing as men effortlessly abseil down billowing sails using nothing but their daggers as support. In this application of the word there is a degree of celebratory, light-hearted heroism attached to it, but originally it only referred to ne'er-do-well louts and uncontrollable rogues (not so far from pirates, incidentally) – in short, losers. It stems from the sixteenth century when it was coined by splicing two older words, swash and buckle. Swash is a verb meaning to run around behaving violently with a sword, and buckle is a shield. Thus, sword and shield are

49

evoked in one compact and sonorous word that evokes the image of battle.

Tickety-boo

If something is tickety-boo it is fine, just right and satisfactory. There are a number of possible origins, none of which is certain. The most often posited explanation is that it is a slang phrase used in the British armed forces from around 1920 onwards. The phrase splices 'that's the ticket' with 'peek-a-boo'. It is easy to make the connection with that's the ticket and tickety-boo, as they have similar meanings, but it is hard to find the logic of combining it with peek-a-boo. In all likelihood, the boo is present merely for euphony, as a pleasing and light-hearted ending to a playful variation on a theme.

Toe the line

To conform, and do as others do. The spelling is definitely toe and not tow: it comes from the military practice of lining up groups of troops for inspection. A good way of assessing if these lines were straight was to ensure that the toes of the men's boots were straight.

CHAPTER FOUR:
NAUTICAL TERMS

Knock Seven Bells

NAUTICAL TERMS

Cut of someone's jib
If you don't like the cut of someone's jib, you don't much like the look of them. The term is nautical: the jib is the triangular-shaped sail found at the front of the boat. The jib was said to be a good indication of what the rest of the ship was like. A well-made jib boded well; a poor one suggested that the boat had not been rigged properly.

Hunky-dory
If something is hunky-dory, it is just fine, perfect and as it should be – 'Everything's

hunky-dory' is perhaps the most common expression containing the phrase. It dates from the nineteenth century and was invented by American sailors who used it to describe a street named Honcho-dori in Yokahoma, Japan. The street used to be well known for the services it provided to lonely sailors, who went there to enjoy what was on offer. It must have taken the linguistic ingenuity of one such sailor to make a connection between the words Honcho and hunky and to invent the punning alternative name for the road, Hunky-dori. The pun would have made sense too, as hunk used also to mean well-being and safety. The new phrase caught on quickly and a sailor who was hunky-dori was happy for one reason or another. Over the years it lost its association with a certain street of vice and what went on there, and took on the much cleaner connotations of general well-being.

In the doldrums
An expression for a directionless state of mind. Sailors have always found that, as the equator is approaching, something weird happens to the

wind. A good strong wind will vanish and instead become calm and directionless. This band of ill weather was termed the doldrums; when ships relied on wind to sail, being in the doldrums meant many weeks of tedious sitting about, aimless boredom and anguished musings. The word is thought to come from the Old English *dol*, meaning dull. The doldrums are now known as the Intertropical Convergence Zone, and the confounding winds are caused by the meeting of the north-east and south-east trade winds.

Knock seven bells
Knocking seven bells out of someone is a nautical expression. Ships use a system of bell-ringing in order to indicate how much of a shift of four hours has passed: the ship's bell is struck once for every half-hour and, after eight bells have struck, the shift is over. To knock seven bells out of someone is to launch such an attack on someone as to nearly finish their shift on the ship of life. Knocking eight bells out of someone would be to kill them.

Limey

This slang word for an Englishman sprang up in the nineteenth century. The British Navy ensured that its seamen were rationed limes in order to prevent scurvy, a disease common on ships that is caused by a lack of vitamin C in the diet. Limey was first a description of an English sailor, but has since been applied to Englishmen in general.

Tide you over

If you are using something to tide you over, you are more than likely going through a period where there is a shortage of one thing or another. That which is tiding you over is sufficient to prevent you from being overwhelmed by the difficulty of a situation. The phrase stems from the image of a rising tide that, as you rise with it, lifts you out of trouble and safely over a challenging or threatening obstacle. The idea of the tide doing the work suggests a lack of need for effort on the part of the lucky benefactor.

True colours

If you show your true colours, you reveal to

others intentions, aspects of your personality or behavioural traits that were hitherto hidden from them. The phrase can be used as praise ('When Harry donated his entire life savings to the local badger hospital, he really showed his true colours, bless him!') but more often tends to be used in a snide and negative way ('When Harry bought the local badger hospital and then burned it for the insurance money and sold the land for a tidy profit, he *really* showed his true colours!'). The phrase derives from an early use of 'colours' to mean flag, pennant or badge. Warships often carried the flags of many nations on board so that they could craftily mislead and elude the enemy – the accepted code of conduct in so-called 'civilised' warfare was for ships to hoist their national flags before entering into battle. If a ship carried many flags, it could deceitfully hail another ship by flying one flag and then hoisting their own once they were in firing range, thus showing their true colours and catching the enemy off guard.

CHAPTER FIVE:
ANIMAL MAGIC

Albertross Around One's Neck

ANIMAL MAGIC

Albatross around one's neck
To have an albatross around one's neck is to be weighed down by something that is hard to escape. It often refers to a past event or action that has negatively affected a person's ability to deal with the present, but it can also be used as a metaphor for anything that is hard to avoid or get away from. The phrase refers to 'The Rime of the Ancient Mariner', by the English poet Samuel Taylor Coleridge. An albatross arrives at the ship while it is stuck in ice, bringing good luck and freeing the vessel. However, the Mariner shoots the albatross and, as a

punishment, its body is hung round his neck. It is not until the Mariner blesses some sea snakes a long time later that the albatross is removed. Coleridge's lesson is clear: respect God's creatures and you will never find the heaviest of birds weighing you down!

Bull and bear markets

Markets in which share prices are, respectively, rising and falling. It is easy to understand how a bull market has come to mean a market whose price is on the up: the bull, an aggressive animal, is a great metaphor for that which is confident and aggressive. However, it is more difficult to see how bears come into the scenario. After all, bears are ferocious and predatory, and not, as far as we know, especially negative creatures. The origin relates to their skins. A hunter would often receive payment for a bearskin before he had hunted and killed it. This type of sale, where the price is fixed before the goods are received, is now called short selling, and it is this kind of sale that is the most common during a bear market: if a trader can fix a price before the shares are sold, it is likely that, by the time the shares are handed over, the price will have dropped.

Come a cropper

This phrase is apt to describe one who is sailing along comfortably when all of a sudden a change in fortune leads them to be brought down to earth with a bump. Indeed, being brought to earth with a bump is precisely the spirit in which the phrase was originally coined. It means to fall headlong, especially from a horse, but nowadays we tend to apply it to general instances of failure. In all likelihood, it is derived from 'neck and crop', meaning completely and thoroughly (crop meaning throat, so the phrase reinforces itself). A neck and crop fall was, in the early nineteenth century, a very bad fall for a horse, and cropper came out of this to mean anything done in a neck and crop fashion.

Dog days

The hot, sticky days of mid- to late summer when the heat gets to people and movement is generally slow. The phrase comes from ancient

Greek astrology. Sirius, the dog star – part of the constellation of Canis Major, the big dog – rises and sets in line with the sun in the northern hemisphere during this late summer period. The ancients believed that it was the heat of the dog star and the heat of the sun combined that made the days so stifling. In fact, it is the tilt of the earth's axis that exposes the northern hemisphere to more of the sun's radiation at this time that makes the days so hot.

Don't buy a pig in a poke

Advice to a purchaser to ensure that you first check the quality of goods before you go ahead and buy them. The origin is thought to date from the 1500s and began as advice to London traders. A poke was a small sack or bag that was used to carry goods to market. Its size made it perfect to carry piglets home. The phrase advises that the buyer first open the sack and inspect the goods within before purchase because market traders could give you a sack containing something else that wriggled but wasn't actually a pig – a stray puppy or a cat for example.

64

Gubbins

If something is a load of old gubbins, whether it be someone's goods, words or thoughts, it is of poor quality, even useless. Frequently used in an affectionately dismissive manner, these days you are more likely to hear a member of an older generation put the phrase to use as it is a rather dated slang expression. In the seventeenth century the Gubbins were the unruly and wild inhabitants of an area in Devon, England, near a place called Brentor. They were so called after the term for the useless and worthless shavings that remain after fish had been scaled – gubbins. So, whether a term for fish bits or uncouth peoples, the prefix 'a load of old' renders the gubbins truly pointless: oldness, in these cases at least, intensifies the sense of the ineffectual.

Guinea pig

To be a guinea pig is to be the subject of someone's experiment. It is also a small, fluffy, domesticated rodent. It is not certain why guinea pigs are so called, but they were widely used in scientific investigations in the nineteenth century.

Hare-brained

If you are hare-brained, you are silly, frivolous, mad even, and most likely an object of ridicule. The confusion that often arises about whether it is a hare or a hair that is referred to in the phrase can be cleared up easily: at the time the expression came about (around 1500) both words were interchangeable spellings for the four-legged furry creature – so cast from your mind all images of brains forged of flowing locks! Quite plainly, the reference to hares relates to mad march hares and their allegedly crazy antics during the mating season. For humans, alas, being hare-brained does not guarantee mates.

Having kittens

This phrase tends to be applied to women who are suffering from an uncontrollable fear. That it is often applied to women gives a clue to its origins. The phrase refers to a uniquely feminine state, pregnancy, and dates back to the medieval belief in the power of witches. Cats have always been closely associated with witches, and it was thought that witches could perform a spell on a pregnant woman by turning her baby into kittens that would scratch at her womb. This macabre understanding arose from what were, in most cases, perfectly normal pregnancy pains. It is possible to imagine the kind of fear that would have gripped the 'victim' in more superstitious times. However, as our superstitions have diminished, we have been left only with this strange image.

Hell for leather

Going 'hell for leather' would describe today the man in the Merc or BMW in the outside lane who flashes his lights at cars that aren't going or can't go at 120 mph. It was originally applied to riding a horse with similar aggression – it would have been hell for the 'leather' of the horse's skin.

Humbug

Humbug is a word that achieved its celebrity status when immortalised in Charles Dickens's festive creation *A Christmas Carol*, and it is used to refer to something that is nonsense, or someone who talks it. For anyone who has somehow managed to escape reading the book or witnessing one of the numerous film and TV adaptations of it, it is the story of the miserly curmudgeon Ebenezer Scrooge who declares Christmas and all the goodwill associated with it to be humbug. An endearing explanation of its origin says that the word referred to a bug by the same name that made a loud humming noise akin to that of a locust or grasshopper. The story goes that this name was picked up and used as a metaphor for something that makes a lot of noise but is rather insignificant. It was first used in the late eighteenth century, and can also be used to mean a person or thing that deceives, which also fits in with the theme of a big noise made by a small creature.

Mad as a march hare

Used to describe a person's eccentric behaviour, this expression is possibly a corruption of an expression by Erasmus, who lived during the late fifteenth and early sixteenth century, and wrote 'as mad as a marsh hare'. Lewis Carroll (1832–98) popularised the modern form 'march hare' in *Through The Looking Glass*, in which the

Cheshire Cat speaks to Alice of a hatter and a hare, both of whom it says are 'mad'. There is a common misapprehension that hares become particularly frenetic during the month of March. In fact, there is no evidence to support the belief that hares go 'mad' at any time of the year. A 1984 study of hares in spring showed that their behaviour then does not differ from that in other months. In other words, the chasing and boxing of females by the males is nothing out of the ordinary – hares, it seems, are always mad!

Monkey's uncle

'I'll be a monkey's uncle' is a phrase employed to express shock, incredulity or just plain surprise. It originated in the 1920s and refers to the theories laid down by Charles Darwin's 1859 work *Origin of Species*. As most of us are at least dimly aware, Darwin pointed out how close we humans are in physical terms to apes and monkeys. The idea that we are descended from our furry friends was scoffed at by many, and the phrase came about as a sarcastic response to it, then slipping into the language to refer to anything unbelievable.

Pigs might fly

Pigs might fly is a wonderfully absurd phrase, steeped in sarcasm, that conjures a stupendous image. It is used humorously to suggest the utter improbability of an event or situation arising. 'I think that this time next year I will have made my fortune selling these balls of string,' a naïve yet wishful thinker might say. 'Yes, and pigs might fly,' would come the ruefully sarcastic response. The idea of flying pigs being linked to preposterous notions originates in a sixteenth-century proverb containing the words 'Pigs flie in the ayre with their tails forward'. The implication is that the likelihood of pigs flying is so small that for them to do so backwards would be just as likely and no more surprising. Some may recall the phrase popping up in Lewis Carroll's *Alice in Wonderland*. Alice asserts her 'right to think' to the Duchess, who promptly responds that she has 'just about as much right ... as pigs have to fly.' Incidently, the Russians use the phrase 'when shrimps whistle' to mean a similar thing.

Sacred cow

An institution or practice that is blindly adhered

to and which hinders progress. The *zebu* cow is a sacred animal in the Hindu religion. The British in India were baffled by the Hindu custom of revering these cows, and this gave rise to the phrase we know today. In fact, of course, cows were highly prized as they provided a means of farming land as well as a crucial source of nourishing milk. The suggestion that their sacred cows be slaughtered would be akin to suggesting to the British that we slaughter our cats and dogs.

Wet behind the ears
To be naïve or lacking in experience. The phrase stems from the state of many farm animals after birth. There is a small indentation behind the ears of calves and lambs which, after birth, takes longer to dry than the rest of their body. There is a variation to this phrase, although it is rarely written or heard: dry behind the ears refers to someone who has acquired a bit of maturity.

CHAPTER SIX:
ANCIENT TIMES

Keeping Your Eyes Peeled

ANCIENT TIMES

Blackball

To vote against someone. At least as far back as Ancient Greece, people have voted by dropping different objects into bags. In many private-members clubs, similar systems have been used for deciding whether or not to elect members into the club. A white ball would signify a yes vote, a black ball a no. Blackballing a candidate was simply voting against them, but its contemporary use is slightly stronger than this, implying a more sustained campaign against an individual.

Caesarean section

A surgical procedure for complicated pregnancies that involves delivering the child by cutting through the mother's abdomen. The term actually comes from the legend that Julius Caesar's own birth was facilitated in this way. Whether or not this is true is not known. *Caesus* in Latin means 'having been cut'. Caesar's mother is thought to have survived the birth of her son, and it seems unlikely that she would have survived such a traumatic procedure in ancient Rome. At any rate, the legend stuck and modern medicine has been happy to perpetuate the myth.

Green with envy

The female poet Sappho described a lover in pain as having a green complexion. This actually represents a Greek idea of physiology where jealousy was thought to make the body produce green bile, which would colour the face green. Some time after Sappho, the idea was made famous again when Shakespeare's character Iago said in *Othello*:

O! beware my lord, of Jealousy;
It is the green-ey'd monster which doth mock
The meat it feeds on.

Hector

To hector somebody is, according to the *Oxford English Dictionary*, a verb meaning to bully by torment or teasing. It is also a noun – a hector is the person doing the hectoring. The word originated in London in the 1800s, when a number of street gangs were causing havoc. They took names such as the Scowerers and the Nickers, and one particularly wild mob of violent men were called the Hectors. Their name refers to the Trojan warrior Hector in Homer's epic poem *The Iliad*. Many may be quick to point out that Hector was no bully, and they would be right – hector only became a noun once the notoriety of the gang led the name to be used to refer to any type of boisterous bully. It is easy to see how the verb to hector grew out of this.

Hippocratic oath

This oath used to be a mandatory part of a

doctor's graduation. The new doctor swears 'by Apollo' to uphold the ethics of a physician: to hold human life sacred and not to abuse his position. Hippocrates, a physician who practised between 460 and 380 BC, is thought to have written the first draft; however, the first time it was known to have been used in a medical school was nearly 2,000 years later in Wittenburg, Germany, in 1508. It did not become a common part of medical graduation until the nineteenth century, when it became commonplace in both European and American medical schools.

Hysterical

The modern sense of the word hysterical denotes helpless mirth, whereas its traditional sense indicates an agitated state that includes dangerously distracted panic, mania and despair. Hysteria was thought to be a condition peculiar to women and the word derives from the Greek *hystero*, meaning 'womb'. Hysteria was thought to be caused by a 'wandering womb'. In order to cure the woman of her condition, the first hysterectomies were performed. In the

Victorian era, new theories speculated that the problems were caused by sexual frustration, and this led to the surprising development of the first vibrators. Hysteria is no longer classified as a disease.

It's all Greek to me

This is a phrase we may utter when utterly unable to understand the language in which something is being spoken, or indeed if we are unable to understand what is being said even if the language is familiar to us – in short, we use it when things just don't make sense. It origins lie in age-old linguistic snobbery and xenophobia. It comes directly from a Latin saying, *Graecum est, non potest legi*, meaning 'It is Greek, it cannot be read'. This was literally the case for Latin speakers, but over the centuries the phrase has come to refer to anything that cannot be understood. The good people of Greece are not known to use the phrase but, if they were to, we can assume they would employ it to express perfect comprehension of a situation.

Janus-faced

Someone who is Janus-faced has two sides to their character. An object can also be said to be Janus-faced if it can be seen in two contrasting ways. Janus was the Roman god of doorways whose name derives from *ianua*, the Latin word for door. He simultaneously stood for the past and future, the reasoning behind this being that doors can be walked through in either direction. To illustrate this, he was always portrayed as having two faces – one looked forward to the future, the other looked back to the past. Celebrated by the Romans, who named January after him and used his name to represent new beginnings, Janus never performed any mythological act to generate our sense of someone who is deceitful – we merely picked up on his two faces, noting the convenient similarity with our already existing expression two-faced. So, Janus never did anything wrong or sly, yet we use his name freely to refer to the double-crossing types who traverse our lives occasionally.

Keep your eyes peeled

This is an instruction dating from the mid-nineteenth century that one person might receive from another to tell them to look out for something with extreme attentiveness. 'I'm keeping my eyes peeled for a signed first edition of *Harry Potter and The Philosopher's Stone*,' we may say as we browse the Internet for rare books. If we conjure up in our minds what the phrase means literally, the result is a pretty grotesque notion of personal injury, and it is hard to imagine how this relates to using one's eyes with any efficiency. However, a brief history of the word peeled clears up this confusion. It is derived from the word pill, which in turn derived from the Latin *pilare*, which means either 'to pluck' or 'to remove the hair'. Over time, the spelling of pill changed to peel and the sense of plucking and removing had morphed into one of removing the outer covering of something. Hence, to keep one's eyes peeled is to figuratively remove any surface layer on the eyes that might hinder a clear view.

Marathon

A race of approximately twenty-six miles. The Battle of Marathon in 490 BC was a crucial point in Greek history. Darius, the Persian King, had amassed an army of 48,000 men at Marathon bay. He outnumbered the Greeks by four to one but, through superior tactics, the Greeks surrounded the Persians and forced them to flee. However, Miltiades, the Greek commander, realised that Athens was still vulnerable to attack by Persian ships if the city's defences were not prepared. The Greek soldier Phidippides was dispatched to run the gruelling twenty-six-mile journey to Athens to warn against the impending Persian assault. It is said that, at the end of the journey, he delivered his message only to drop dead from exhaustion (he had been fighting all day, after all).

Minutes of a meeting

You would be forgiven for thinking that the minutes of a meeting are so called because they detail a meeting minute by minute. In fact, the phrase refers to how minutes were first written. The word is from the Latin *minutia*, meaning 'smallness'. The events of a meeting were written in small script at the meeting; when copies were distributed to relevant parties, the small minutes were 'engrossed' – written out in a larger, more legible script.

Platonic love

The philosopher Plato lent his name to this form of love that prefers to keep itself at arm's length. The Italian Renaissance scholar Marsilio Ficino used the term *amor platonicus* to describe a form of love described in Plato's *Symposium* where, rather than cultivating sexual passion, a union of souls was formed through pure intellectual pursuit. The phrase still refers to non-physical love and has become a substitute for saying 'just good friends'; however, it is doubtful whether many modern Platonic friends could be bothered to aim quite as high as Plato would have done.

Pyrrhic victory

A victory that has been won at too high a cost to bring any advantage, and is thus empty and meaningless. From 280 to 279 BC King Pyrrhus of Epirus led an army of 20 elephants and 30,000 men against the Romans in southern Italy. He won many battles against the Romans, but lost so many men that he eventually had to retreat. After one such battle he is said to have declared, 'Another victory like that and I shall be ruined!'

Quid pro quo

This legal phrase entered usage in the sixteenth century to refer to a reciprocal exchange of goods or services. Literally translated from Latin it means 'something for something'.

Quidnunc

An obscure word to describe a gossip. Literally translated from the Latin it means 'what now' – the idea being that a quidnunc is someone who always asks, 'What now?', eager to find out the latest gossip.

Sapphic love

Homosexual love between two women. The term comes from the early seventh-century Greek poetess Sappho. She lived on the island of Lesbos, which, through association with Sappho, has given us the word lesbian. Little remains of her poetry other than a few fragments, many of which contain vivid and intense poems to female lovers. It is believed that Sappho ran and taught in a school for young, wealthy women, where she would have found a great deal of inspiration for her poetry.

The die is cast

This phrase is used to tell someone to stop worrying about the outcome of something. There's nothing they can do about any more. Julius Caesar is traditionally said to have coined the phrase (in Latin *alea iacta est*) when he led the Roman army into Italy to seize power.

CHAPTER SEVEN:
SPORTS AND GAMES

Birdie

SPORTS AND GAMES

Ace in the hole
If you have an ace in the hole, you have a hidden advantage. The expression is derived from poker terminology. A 'hole' card is one that isn't revealed until all bets have been made. An ace is the highest-scoring card in poker.

Aerobics
The idea of aerobic exercise was created by Dr Kenneth Cooper. The word is based on Greek and means 'air life'. Essentially, aerobic exercise is sustained activity that results in an increase in breathing and an increased heart rate. This

pumps blood into the muscles being exercised. Dr Cooper's book *Aerobics* was published in 1968.

Albatross

The completion of a hole of golf in three strokes under par. It is so named because the albatross is an even larger bird than the eagle, and even more rare – rather like making three under par.

At sixes and sevens

To be confused. The expression dates back to medieval England and is used in Chaucer's *Troilus and Criseyde* in around 1380. The original expression was probably from a gambling expression 'set at six and seven'. The phrase was used to describe a situation where a gambler staked all his possessions on the six and 'seven' of the die – the six as a high number was seen as an unlikely throw, and of course the 'seven' was impossible on a six-sided die, so the phrase described an improbable or foolhardy bet. Over time this became associated with the befuddlement that can sometimes beset a gambler, and over even more time it has come to mean only the confusion itself.

Birdie

The completion of a hole of golf in one stroke under par. 'Bird' was once a word rather like 'cool' is today. The story goes that a certain Ab Smith, a golfer of some reputation, was playing golf with his acquaintances in Atlantic City in 1899. His ball came to rest just inches near the hole leaving him one under par. 'That was a bird of a shot!' he cried, and he and his acquaintances decided to describe scores of one under par as 'birdies'.

Blue-chip

Blue-chip companies are those that are particularly reliable and likely to provide a steady return on one's investments. The term comes from poker – blue poker chips have the highest values. The association of multinationals with poker is either ironic or entirely apt, depending on your point of view.

Bogey

The completion of a hole of golf in one stroke over par. Bogey is British in origin. 'Colonel Bogey' was a popular tune that was around in the 1890s. Although now best known for lyrics concerning Adolf Hitler, the original song contained the line 'I'm the bogeyman, catch me if you can.' The bogeyman was the elusive character of the song, and playing a bogey was a reminder that the elusive par you wanted had slid just out of reach. An alternative theory, similar in theme, is suggested by the *Oxford English Dictionary*: bogey was a nineteenth-century word for the Devil, who was deemed to be an imaginary player on the golf course.

Caddy

Caddy is derived from the French *le cadet* meaning the youngest boy. It is similar in derivation to the English word cadet.

Derby

This is a name given to an annual horse race. The story goes that the twelfth Duke of Derbyshire was dining with his pal Sir Charles Bunbury when they decided to organise a race for three-year-old fillies at Epsom, and that the name of the race was decided on the toss of coin – the duke won. The race took place on 4 May 1780, and Bunbury's horse Diomed came first. (*See also Local derby*)

Drongo

Australian slang meaning a stupid or useless person. The original drongo was a racehorse in the 1920s. The horse was frequently tipped as a possible winner, but throughout his unfortunate career Drongo never managed a win. After his retirement, racing writers would describe a horse who had never quite fulfilled its potential as a drongo. Gradually the name became a form of insult for someone who was considered a loser.

Duck

In cricket, as any batsman knows, a duck is what you get if you are bowled out without scoring. A golden duck is what you get if you are bowled out on the first ball you face, and to break a duck is to score the first run of your innings. This peculiar term comes from the idea that a duck's egg resembles a zero. The term has mutated in America into the phrase 'to lay an egg', which is applied to any poorly scoring sporting achievement.

Eagle

The completion of a hole of golf in two strokes

under par. As its value is greater than that of a birdie, the shot is given the name of a 'great' bird.

Fore!

It is not absolutely certain where this shout to beware of errant golf balls comes from, but it is most likely that it was an abbreviation of the cry 'Forecaddy!' Forecaddies were employed to stand down the fairway so that they could find balls that went missing.

Get one's goat

This is a twentieth-century American phrase relating to horse racing. It used to be common practice at horse races for goats to be used in order to keep restless horses under control – they had a calming effect on the horse and this made it all the more race-ready. On race days, goats were stolen ('got') by wily thieves who, expecting the horse to be distressed by the absence of its bearded mentor, would then place a bet on it to lose. Today, if something or someone gets your goat, it annoys, distresses and irritates you, as if you were a horse whose goat had been got by something.

Get the ball rolling

This is ideally suited to the vocabulary of the middle manager as it refers to team sports. Getting the ball rolling is what you need to begin a ball game of any kind. The phrase has become a metaphor for the beginning of any team activity and works as a stock cliché to begin meetings with.

Great white hope

A great white hope is something that is going to come along and change fortunes for the better. Although anyone using it today won't be accused of opening up a racial divide, racial divides are very much at the root of the expression. In 1908, a black American heavyweight boxer, Jack Johnson, beat white Canadian opponent Tommy Burns. This was regarded as a terrible blow to white superiority and an American boxer, James Jeffries, came out of retirement to become the 'great white hope' of Caucasian America. Johnson beat him in 1910, sparking violence against African-Americans across the country. A great white hope came to mean any boxer who could overturn black superiority in boxing. While this is no longer a contentious issue in the sport, the phrase has persisted to symbolise a person or idea upon which many hopes are pinned.

Have a flutter

A flutter is usually a small bet placed in a casual way, as opposed to a large bet placed in a wild-eyed, pencil-snapping frenzy. The phrase 'How about a flutter?' has a similar resonance with the gambler as 'Fancy a pint?' does for those who enjoy a drink a little too much. The expression derives from the quivering state of anticipation known up and down racecourses throughout the globe once a bet has been placed and the race is about to begin.

High jinks

Boisterous and unruly fun. High jinks was originally a drinking game especially popular in Scotland from around the eighteenth century. The 'jinks' part of the phrase is an old word for a darting movement made by someone to get out of the way. In the game, a die was thrown and, depending on the score, a forfeit was administered to the player. They had the choice of drinking more and risking embarrassing inebriation or performing the forfeit, which was unlikely to be dignified. It is easy to see how the name of the game has become a description of the kind of playful anarchy now associated with high jinks.

Knocked for six

This phrase is usually applied to someone who has received a great shock, although it is sometimes applied to the loser of brawl. The maximum points you can score from a bowler's delivery in cricket is six runs, and to do this the batsman must hit the ball out of the pitch's boundary without it touching the ground. So, to be knocked for six is to have the maximum damage done to you in one go.

Local derby

In football, when two teams from the same town play each other, the match is known as a derby. Often this requires extra security measures to be taken by the police and the game itself will be particularly competitive. The origin of the term derives from a football match that was begun between two parishes of the town of Ashbourne, near Derby, over Shrove Tuesday. It was, and still is, a violent affair – even today it causes shops to board up their windows. The 'pitch' is three miles long, and the rules do not resemble those of conventional football: for example, handling the ball is permitted. Edward III tried to ban it in 1349 on the grounds that it interfered with his archery practice, and there have been a number of deaths throughout the game's long history. While not actually held in Derby itself, the town is near enough to have lent its name to the occasion, and to other conventional football matches that have a similarly keen sense of rivalry.

Mexican wave

This is a truly marvellous sight to see or be part of in any stadium. A Mexican wave occurs when spectators stand up and sit down in sequence, and it came to prominence during the 1986 World Cup, which was held in Mexico. Before then, it was popular in the Americas, although, like the wave itself, it is rather difficult to say exactly when or where it began.

On your tod

If you are on your tod, you are alone, either physically or metaphorically in, say, your opinions or beliefs. The phrase owes itself to the life of one James Todhunter Sloan, a hugely popular and skilful American jockey. At his peak, he rode for the Prince of Wales in 1895. He famously invented the technique of riding one's horse using short stirrups and bending over so one's head is very near the head of the horse, and when not racing led a wild life of socialising and gambling away vast amounts of money (he also earned vast sums, so it posed no problem!). His good fortune ran out at the turn of the century when his application for a licence from the Jockey Club of Great Britain was rejected on the grounds of his inappropriate behaviour tarnishing the image of the sport. The Americans and the French followed suit in denying him licences, which meant that he was reduced instantly to an impotent force. The good times were over for James Todhunter Sloan, who became a shadow of his former self, eventually dying in 1933, destitute and alone, of liver disease. Out of this tragic fall grew a cockney rhyming slang term, to be on your Tod Sloan (on your own). On your tod is the shortened version.

Pass the buck

To pass the responsibility for something on to someone else, often in an underhand way. In poker terminology, a buck is a marker that signifies which player is in charge of the bank. Passing the buck, then, was handing over the responsibility of the bank to someone else. This terminology slipped into the world of the office, where memos were passed around with a buck slip, on to which was written a list of all the relevant people who were to read the memo. The slip was passed around, and staff were expected to tick their names off as they read it. A way of putting off acting on the memo would be to 'pass the buck', or hand the slip on without ticking off your name. Assuming that eventually the office did get round to ticking off all their names, the buck slip would stop being passed around – the buck stopped there! Whatever was in the memo, therefore, would have to be enacted.

Stumped

To be at a total loss. You might think that the origin of this word would be part of cricketing terminology – to be 'stumped' in cricket is when the batsman has the bails knocked off his cricket stumps, usually by the wicket keeper. The batsman is then out. However, the origin of the phrase is actually American. Land that had not been cleared properly would sometimes have a number of tree stumps in the middle of a field. Anyone ploughing the field would soon find their activities 'stumped' by the number of tree stumps getting in the way of the plough.

The chips are down

Things are looking grim or unsteady, and it is necessary to make some bold decisions. The phrase is directly lifted from gambling terminology. At the end of a heavy evening, a player might find that luck has not been with him: he has lost a lot of money and therefore his gambling chips were 'down' to the last few.

Throw in the towel

Meaning to give up after a long struggle, to

admit defeat, this phrase finds its origin in the boxing ring. In the mid-nineteenth century, if a boxer could be seen to be fighting a losing battle, then his seconds were entitled to throw an object into the ring to acknowledge on his behalf that their man was defeated. More often than not, the closest item to hand would have been the sponge used to clean the fighter off between rounds, so the phrase to 'throw up the sponge' came into use. As boxing, and language, practices changed, it duly became throw in the towel.

Turn the tables

Turning the tables produces a reversal in fortunes for opponents. The phrase seems to have its origins in board games. In the seventeenth century, backgammon was known in England as 'tables', and there existed a rule that allowed the opponents to 'turn tables' and play the opponent's position. Another suggestion is that it may have come from chess, where the two players agree to turn the board around and continue to play their opposite colours in order to make the game more interesting.

CHAPTER EIGHT:
PLACES

Place In The Sun

PLACES

Bedlam

A place where madness and chaos reign. Bedlam was a hospital established in 1247 and properly called St Mary of Bethlehem. It was originally on the site of what is now Liverpool Street Station in London. Over the centuries the hospital dealt exclusively with the insane, and the name Bethlehem became truncated to Bedlam. In the 1700s it was opened to the public and it is estimated that the hospital had around 100,000 visitors every year.

Belfast

A fort was built by the Anglo-Normans in the twelfth century. Around the fifteenth century it became known in Gaelic as Beal Feirste, which means 'approach to the sandspit' (a sandspit is a narrow strip of sand that projects into a body of water), so the name is really a geographical description of the original port area of the city. Belfast is simply the anglicised pronunciation of the name.

Bethlehem

The Hebrew *bêth lehem* means 'house of bread'. It is, of course, also the birthplace of Jesus Christ, who emphasised the ritual breaking of bread as the focus of the Christian communion. Given the nature of God and His mysterious workings, this is unlikely to be simple coincidence. Indeed, the book of Micah in the Old Testament contains a prophecy that Bethlehem would be the birthplace of the Messiah: 'But you, O Bethlehem Eph'rathah, who are little to be among the clans of Judah, from you shall come forth for me one who is to be ruler in Israel, whose origin is from of old, from ancient days' (Micah 5:1-6). Interestingly, in Arabic, *bêt lahm*, means 'house of meat'.

Blarney

To talk blarney is not just to talk nonsense. Blarney is a particular form of nonsense peculiar to Ireland: a spontaneous combination of lyricism, punning, strange leaps of logic and other verbal tricks goes into the mix to produce a humorous, baffling monologue that will often leave the listener none the wiser, sometimes benignly deceived but much entertained. If the legendary Blarney stone at Blarney Castle near Cork is kissed, the kisser is said to be bequeathed the gift of the gab. The word was supposedly coined by Elizabeth I. Dermot McCarthy of Blarney Castle kept promising to surrender the place to the Queen as a demonstration of his loyalty. However, whenever pressed, he managed to evade the issue. On one such occasion, she is said to have exclaimed, 'Odds bodikins, more Blarney talk!'

Cardiff

Cardiff is an Anglicisation of its Welsh name,

Caerdydd. It is not entirely certain how the name came into being. *Caer* is a fort or castle in Welsh, but the 'dydd' part of the name doesn't seem to make sense. It could be a corruption of 'taff' – the river Taff runs through the city, and the letter d in Welsh often translates as a t in English. It is more likely that it is named after a Roman commander, Aulus Didius, who established a fort there during the Roman occupation.

Dublin

Dublin was officially founded by the Vikings in AD 988, although there is evidence that the site was occupied in one form or another as far back as the Mesolithic age (11000–9000 BC). Its original Gaelic name was Baile Átha Cliath, which means 'the town of Hurdle Ford'. Hurdle Ford was an ancient bridge that crossed the river Liffey. When the Vikings moved in, the town became known as Dyfflin or Dubh Linn, meaning 'black pool'. This was because, at the place where the river Poddle joined the Liffey, a deep, dark pool was formed in which it was easier to land ships.

Edinburgh

A fort and small settlement was established during the Bronze Age between 1500 and 1000 BC by the Picts on the site of what is now Holyrood Park. Around the time of the Roman occupation, the Gododdin tribe are thought to have named the place Dun Eidyn, meaning simply 'hill fort'. The town was never captured by the Romans, and it is one of the sites in Europe that has undergone the longest continual occupation. After it was attacked by the Bernician Angles in the sixth century, its name was changed to Edinburh – *burh* meaning town. The spelling was later modernised to Edinburgh.

Elephant and Castle

Elephant and Castle is a south London district most famous for its huge roundabout and dilapidated pink shopping centre. Its peculiar name was copied from that of a sixteenth-century playhouse that staged many of Shakespeare's plays, the Newington Theatre. The theatre was converted into a tavern in the eighteenth century, and a model of an elephant and a castle was situated at the front of the establishment, which was demolished in 1959. The model was kept, though, and is now displayed at the pink shopping centre. The elephant on the sign was the emblem of the Cutler's Company, who appropriated it when company members wore elephant decorations on their coats at the marriage of Henry VI and Queen Margaret in 1445. The elephants symbolised the ivory used by cutlers in their trade. Many people falsely claim that Elephant and Castle is a version of *Infanta de Castile*, which references Eleanor of Castile, the wife of Edward I.

Hong Kong

What is now Hong Kong didn't really come into being until the Opium War of 1839–42 between England and China. The island was of strategic importance from a trading point of view because its deep harbour provided a safe hub from which to trade. The island also contained what had once been plantations of the Hueng tree, the leaves of which were used to make incense. The British named the place from the Chinese Hueng Gong, which can be translated as fragrant harbour.

Los Angeles

Los Angeles' story begins at what was the American Indian village Yang Na, which was located near where the city's civic centre stands today. Gaspar de Portolá arrived at the village on 2 August 1769 and, because the date was the feast day of Our Lady of Angels, he named the river Nuestra Señora de los Angeles de la Porciúncula (Our Lady of the Angels of the Little Portion). The little portion describes a parcel of land near Assisi in Italy on which stood a chapel that was given to Francis of Assisi by Benedictine monks. The chapel apparently contained a fresco of the Virgin Mary surrounded by angels. The feast day on 2 August celebrated the chapel. Several years later, in 1781, a settlement was established along the river and named after it. In time this unwieldy name was abbreviated to Los Angeles. Interestingly, many of the cities along the west coast of America have Spanish names because the Spanish led the first expeditions from

Europe up that side of the country. The British pretty much controlled all of the eastern seaboard up to what is now Canada, and so the names of towns and cities there tend to be English or American Indian in origin.

Manchester

What is Manchester today began life as a Roman fort on the plateau of a hill about a mile south of where the cathedral now stands. The Romans called the hill Mamuciam (breast shaped), and the fort and civilian settlement existed until the Romans left in AD 407. In the seventh century, the Saxons created a new settlement there. They called any former Roman town *caester* and the new town became know as Mamm caester. Later the spelling was modernised to Manchester.

Mecca

Mecca has come to mean a place that attracts thousands of people. Paris, for example, is a Mecca for shoppers. The original Mecca was founded when Abraham left his wife Hagar and his son Ishmael in the valley of Mecca, in what is now the capital of Saudi Arabia. At the time the valley was barren desert. Commanded to do so by Allah, Abraham reluctantly abandoned his wife and child to the elements. Miraculously, water sprang from Ishmael's feet, just at the point when Hagar had begun to despair over her and her child's fate. The city flourished from that point. In around AD 570 Mohammed, the prophet and founder of Islam, was born there. The city had already become a centre of pilgrimage by that point, and has become perhaps the greatest place of pilgrimage in the world. In the 1980s, the Saudi Arabian government encouraged the spelling Makkah to be used when referring to the geographical place, leaving Mecca for the metaphorical usage.

New York
New York was originally called New Amsterdam and was created in 1625 when the Dutch built a church and a fort on the then Native American territory of Manhattan. The following year, it was said to have been either purchased or leased from the Canarsie tribe by one Peter Minuit for sixty guilders. In 1664 the

British captured Manhattan and called it New York in honour of James Stuart, Duke of York. He was the second son of Charles I, and eventually became James II in 1685.

Paris
The name of the city is derived from the people who first settled there around the third century BC. They were Celtic and known as the *Parisii*, which means 'boat people'. They were successful as river traders, and it is believed that they built a fortified town somewhere on the Ile de la Cité – the island on the Seine where the cathedral of Notre Dame stands today. In 51 BC, the inhabitants participated in the ultimately unsuccessful uprising against Julius Caesar. The Romans referred to the settlement as Lutetia Parisiorum, which approximates to 'the mud city of the Parisii'. Lutetia Parisiorum expanded rapidly under the Romans and, in AD 212, it was wisely decided to drop the mud bit and just call the city Paris.

Place in the sun
When we speak of finding a place in the sun, we

are usually referring to a forthcoming holiday (or the need for one!), or to a property haven in a hot climate that we dream of owning (or, if we are lucky, already own). It is also used to refer to a chance of advancement that is rightfully ours – after many years of service, a hard worker may find their place in the sun when made partner in a company, for instance. The expression has its roots in the struggle of many late-nineteenth-century colonial empires to get their place in the sun through intense exploration and colonisation of what were then seen as 'uncivilised' continents such as Africa and Asia. In 1897, German chancellor Bernard von Bülow, speaking of his country's desire to expand its empire in both the East and Africa, said, 'We desire to throw no one into the shade, but we demand our own place in the sun.' The term was also applied to the pleasure-seeking trend for European citizens to take their holidays in the sunny colonies of the southern hemisphere. These places were associated with prestige, good income and, of course, fine holidays! The phrase stuck and its meaning has now widened to refer to any pleasant spot.

Third World

The term Third World is used to describe developing countries and originated during the Cold War, as did First World and Second World. Surprisingly, though, Third World was coined first. It was translated from the French *le tiers monde* by American and British politicians, who then went on to coin First World, which referred to capitalist countries, and Second World, which referred to communist states.

Tokyo

Tokyo was for many years known as Edo. European reports of the place from the sixteenth century tell us that it was a small, prospering fishing town. However, in 1603 Tokugawa Ieyasu established his government there. Under the warlord the town rapidly grew in size. In 1638 Japan closed its borders to all trade; remarkably, Edo seemed to flourish all the more, and it is thought that by the end of the 1600s its population had grown to over a million. In 1868 the capital of Japan was moved from Kyoto to Edo and the city was renamed Tokyo, which means 'eastern capital'.

CHAPTER NINE:
SARTORIAL MATTERS

Eat One's Hat

SARTORIAL MATTERS

A stitch in time saves nine

A stitch in time saves nine is the kind of thing that mothers tell their children in an effort to persuade them to do things ahead of time. The phrase springs from the situation where a tear in an item of clothing occurs. It is always best to repair the damage at the time, rather than wait until the tear worsens and more work will be required.

Bikini

A female swimsuit with an interesting etymological history! The island of Bikini was devastated in 1946 by American military nuclear testing. That summer, Jacques Heim and Louis Reard both premiered a daring new swimsuit in Cannes. Both claimed to have invented it, and it left rather less to the male imagination than the general populous was used to. With the nuclear test very much in the news, the unfortunate island lent its name to the new apparel: the effect the swimsuit had on the male psyche was thought to be similar to the effect thermonuclear devices had on the island of Bikini.

Bloomers
Bloomers were in fact an early form of feminine trouser. They were popularised by Amelia Jenks Bloomer who advocated them in her monthly New York temperance newspaper *The Lily*. The original bloomers were usually worn under a skirt that reached at least to the knees, and the bloomers themselves were gathered at the ankles, although they weren't necessarily quite as blousy as our picture of them is now. They neatly replaced the acres of underskirts a woman was expected to wear in the nineteenth

century. As bicycling became popular, they were found to be the answer to allowing a lady more freedom to pedal while not exposing her to the grave danger this activity once posed to a woman's modesty. Over time, the bloomers shrank in length to become the undergarment with which we are now more familiar. With the advent of knickers and modern lingerie, bloomers became the kind of thing your auntie wore; they were once, however, the last word in feminist chic.

Bluestocking

A rather obscure term nowadays, bluestocking is the name given to an intellectual woman, and it is usually derogative. The name comes from the mid-eighteenth century when a society of men and woman came together at Elizabeth Montague's Mayfair home in London to talk about the most current cultural topics of the day and to avoid the frivolous gossip that pervaded most of London's gatherings. One member of this elite group, whose conversation was said to especially sparkle, was Benjamin Stillingfleet, who was famed for his sober attire, which he offset by wearing a pair of blue stockings. When Stillingfleet was absent, Montague would comment, 'We can do nothing without the blue stockings.' It is thought that the group began to wear blue stockings to emulate Stillingfleet, and so their nickname was born.

Catwalk

The raised narrow platform that is described as a catwalk is so called simply because cats are renowned for walking along raised narrow platforms!

Eat one's hat

To eat one's hat, theoretically a most unpleasant and difficult task, would no doubt prove to be achievable, yet horrid, in practice. For this reason, people reserve the expression for use in situations where they are utterly convinced of a particular outcome – usually the certainty of something *not* happening, as in statements such as 'If you manage to persuade Granddad to resume his former glorious career as a hurdler, I'll eat my hat!' The phrase was invented by Charles Dickens, who used it in *The Pickwick*

Papers (1836): 'If I knew as little of life as that, I'd eat my hat.' It is hard to say why Dickens chose a hat for the object to be consumed – it was probably just a product of his fertile sense of absurdity and knack of creating striking images that sank into the public consciousness.

Flea market

The phrase seems to have originated through allusion to a famous nineteenth-century market in Paris, *le Marche aux Puces*. Its literal translation is 'the market of fleas'. Popular and cheap, it was renowned for the fact that, were you to buy a garment from one of its many clothes stalls, you would get more than you bargained for in the form of fleas.

Greenhorn

By calling somebody a greenhorn we mean they are amateurish, a trainee or far from an expert in a certain area or skill. One explanation suggests that the phrase originated in the fifteenth century and derives from the fact that young oxen have green horns. A more diverting possibility is the suggestion that the origin can be dated to the seventeenth century and the then thriving world of jewellery manufacture. A certain type of brooch was made out of horn that was set into a silver frame. Decorating the horn was a figure, usually a head, which was pressed into the horn by a delicate process involving careful heating of the horn before shaping it over a mould. The temperature had to be just right, and if it was too high then the horn would end up green instead of the desired brown. To master this process required skill and practice, so the apprentices were named greenhorns and the phrase stuck, over time coming to be applied more broadly so that the original sense was lost.

Have one's work cut out

To have one's work cut out is, in our modern understanding of the phrase, to be facing a large task. The expression is often used to imply that it may, in fact, be unrealistic for a particular job to be completed or a mission achieved. We might say of a husband discovered to be cheating by his wife, 'Well, if he's going to get back in her good books, he's got his work cut out.' The phrase originated in tailoring in the seventeenth century. If one was a practitioner of the trade, then to prepare one's materials and patterns before putting a suit together was to have all one's work cut out. Here, the phrase does not imply the daunting sense of a tough challenge; rather it is an expression of ordered efficiency. The modern sense developed in a transitional period when the phrase came to mean work cut out (ie given) by one person to another. And as many will understand, when people delegate, they often do so rather too enthusiastically. By the 1940s, the phrase was applied to any situation where the pressure is on.

Hoodwink

To be hoodwinked is to be tricked or conned. The phrase comes from a much older sense of the word wink. In the sixteenth century, to wink meant to have the eyes completely closed. To be hoodwinked was to have your head covered by a hood so that you couldn't see – the hood in this case was doing the winking for you. Being tricked and conned is a form of social blindness, and hence the meaning of the term.

125

Jumper

A jumper is an article of clothing worn on the top half of the body, but it seems different people have different ideas about what exactly a jumper is. According to the *Oxford English Dictionary* it can be a 'knitted pullover', a 'loose outer jacket of canvas worn by sailors' or a 'pinafore dress', the latter being an American term. Whichever garment you understand jumper to refer to, its origins are in the mid-1900s and have nothing to do with jumping! The word stems from the Old French *juppe*, meaning 'petticoat', which was adopted as a British dialect term 'jump' to refer to a short coat worn by a man or underclothes worn by a woman. Even though these are quite different senses of the same word, the idea of additional garments specifically designed to give extra warmth is consistent, and as the meaning of the word developed in Britain it was increasingly associated with upper-body garments made from wool for either sex. In America, jumper tends to be an article of women's clothing.

126

Keep your pants on!
This appeal for calm is originally sexual in nature — advice to the heated or flustered individual that sexual activity is not imminent and therefore excitement would be best contained.

Nit-picking
Nit-picking, meaning to find small faults and to criticise over tiny matters, is a figurative phrase deriving from the act of removing lice and their eggs from a person's hair. A difficult, time-consuming task that demands perseverance and careful attention, it is an age-old activity born of unfortunate necessity. The phrase nit-picking has been in use since the first century but, despite the rather self-evident link between the literal and figurative uses of the phrase, the latter sense has only been in use since the beginning of the twentieth century.

Seamy side of life
The seamy side of life is that which we would rather keep away from, or keep hidden. It is the seamy aspects of existence that remind us how

imperfect the world is. The saying has its roots in upholstery and tailoring. If we turn furniture upside down, or clothing inside out, a rougher, less finished and presentable 'side' is revealed to us – the seams. The analogy is simple and effective.

Sock it to them

Sock to them, or sock it to me, is used in several contexts, but the general gist of the phrase is that it is always used as some form of encouragement, either in an aggressive or a supportive way. We might be told to 'sock' a football to a nervous goalkeeper, or others may thrill in watching us (having willed our opponent on with the phrase) have a punch socked to us in the boxing ring; we might encourage a nervous speaker to 'sock it to 'em' just before she enters a room full of ideological adversaries; and, if slightly unhinged or under stress, we may even speak the words to ourselves *sotto voce*, in hushed yet emphatic tones. The phrase, though now used in the USA more than in the UK, derives from the seventeenth-century English usage of the phrase 'to give someone sock', meaning to give someone a good whipping. The word sock was also used to mean hitting someone hard, or attacking them. This tallies perfectly with the current sense of the phrase always being associated with aggressive, or at least decisive and winning, action. The problem is that history offers no real clues as to why the word sock became synonymous with hitting in the first place. There is of course the implication that socks were in some way used to give beatings, but exactly how is a mystery that is begging to be solved. If anyone has any ideas, the author would be grateful if they would sock it to him – but gently, please!

Toerag

The insulting label toerag originates in the 1900s. Street-dwellers and tramps were often seen to wrap pieces of cloth around their feet as a desperate and cheap alternative to socks. The image was quickly seized upon by the educated classes who, finding the practice distasteful, adopted the word toerag and used it to dismissively refer to anyone of shabby appearance and inferior status. Nowadays, the phrase is a choice insult reserved for despicable characters, although it can also be used affectionately.

Well heeled

The term well heeled is used to refer to someone both well off and well dressed. Often thought to be the opposite of down at heel, its origins actually lie in cockfighting. If a bird was well heeled, it was in possession of good spurs – sharp and dangerous metal 'heels' attached to the back of a cock's foot. The better the spurs, the more damage could be done. The phrase also cropped up in America and was used to describe someone armed with a gun. Today our understanding of the word refers to someone with plenty of money and clothes that reflect it. As we all know, wealth is itself a forceful weapon, and thus the original sense endures today.

CHAPTER TEN:
LAW AND (dis) ORDER

The Long Arm Of The Law

LAW AND (dis) ORDER

As well be hanged for a sheep as a lamb
This phrase originated in the eighteenth century when the punishment for the stealing of livestock was execution by hanging. It did not matter, therefore, which type of animal one thieved. The idea, then, is that, if you are going to be punished whatever your actions, you might as well be punished for the more serious crime – in the case of sheep and lambs, it is obvious that the larger animal represents a more valuable acquisition. Today, the expression is used in anticipation of performing an action whose outcome may result in 'punishment'. It is

often used to comment on a present state of
affairs to indicate that one is already in trouble
enough, so there's no harm in continuing the
fun! When asked if they would like another
drink, for instance, a person might accept,
knowing they're going to be hungover
anyway – 'Oh go on then,' they may say, 'I
might as well be hanged for a sheep as a lamb.'

Bobby

This is a slightly old-fashioned slang word for a
police officer, and many of us will associate it
with the phrase bobby on the beat. Policemen
came to be bobbies because of Sir Robert Peel,
the nineteenth-century Tory politician. During
his time as Britain's home secretary, he famously
breathed new life into the London police force.
He did such a good job that the new officers
were nicknamed peelers, but this was soon
enough replaced by the more genial-sounding
bobbies, Bobby being a casual form of the
name Robert.

Cold turkey

The process of kicking an addictive drug habit.

If you happen to put your body through an immediate withdrawal of heroin, one of the symptoms is goose bumps, causing the skin to resemble that of a plucked turkey. In addition, the skin of a withdrawing addict often emits a lot of heat, making the person feel cold. While the phrase is commonly applied to drug addicts, it has slipped down into more common usage to describe kicking any bad habit.

Cop
A policeman. The word cop comes from the now forgotten English word 'cap' meaning seize – similar to capture. A cop was someone who went around seizing people. The longer version, copper, came later and became more common when New York police sergeants carried metallic copper badges as identification.

Cop out
Most of us rightly understand the phrase to cop out as being an expression for backing down or backing out of something. The term, along with the noun cop-out, has connotations of cowardice or weak will on the part of the

135

'copper-outer', yet the history of the phrase reveals its meaning to have undergone several nuances of change. In mid-nineteenth-century England, cop meant to steal, or take (this sense of the word lives on in phrases like 'cop a feel' and 'cop a look'), and cop out grew from this, meaning to have something for yourself. In the interwar years, another sense of cop emerged to describe what policemen often do – catch people, that is! – and the phrase cop out developed into an admission of guilt. Over the years this grew further to mean a confession in any situation. It is easy to see how the sense of giving up, or backing down, inherent in making a confession, carried the phrase forward until it came to be used as we understand it today.

Footloose and fancy-free

Free from emotional and social commitments. The word footloose was coined in the seventeenth century to describe a sense of being free of shackles about the feet – presumably first describing the freedom of bound prisoners. Later it progressed to mean freedom of emotion and action. The word 'fancy' in its original context aligned it closely with love, so to be 'fancy-free' was to be free of the shackles of love. While fancy is emotionally milder these days, the idea of fancying a person still contains strong connotations of emotion.

Frogmarch
To restrain a prisoner's hands and forcibly lead them somewhere. In these enlightened times, however, policemen have to be careful with their prisoners, and so the word is perhaps more commonly used to describe how an angry parent might collect an errant child from some terrible scene of adolescent delinquency. In fact, delinquency plays an important part in the word's history. In the latter half of the nineteenth century, when drunks were so incapacitated that they could only be transported (or rather ejected) from wherever they were, each limb would be held by somebody so that the unfortunate inebriate, splayed out, resembled a frog.

Gerrymander
Gerrymandering is a word now most commonly

used by one politician to accuse another of underhand manipulation of a political situation. Originally it meant to tamper with constituency boundaries in order to ensure that one party got more votes. The phrase actually dates from 1812 and was coined by a cartoonist named Gilbert Stuart. The democrat governor of Massachusetts, Elbridge Gerry, had rearranged the boundaries of the state to help boost his fortunes in the coming elections. Gilbert Stuart deftly added some additional detail to the map to produce something resembling a salamander and he dubbed his creation a 'Gerrymander'. It soon became the word of choice for this kind of politicking, and has survived to this day.

Grass

A grass is someone who has grassed on another, meaning that they have informed on them to an authority (in schools, teachers, in the real world, police) and, in short, landed them in trouble of some sort. A typical grass will not grass without motive, be it financial, personal or merely to save their own bacon. There are two possible origins. The first relates to a 1940 song by the Ink Spots, who achieved international fame and glamour with their hit 'Whispering Grass'. According to this theory, the associations in the song led to whispering becoming known as grassing. The second explanation asserts that someone who regularly informed on criminals to the police (the cop shop, in slang form) became known as a shopper. This was adapted in rhyming slang to become grasshopper, and over time this was shortened to grass. You choose!

In cold blood

To do something in cold blood is to perform an act dispassionately and without emotion. Moreover, the act performed is something that is normally associated with high emotion and passion. A hackneyed phrase, familiar to us all, is cold-blooded murder, which perfectly illustrates the expression's dynamic. Dating from the early eighteenth century, the expression came about due to a belief that a person's blood heated up in moments of anger, exertion and stress. This conclusion was drawn from observations of the body (especially the face) reddening under certain circumstances. So, quite simply, one who could commit a heinous crime and remain calm both physically and emotionally was said to be acting in cold blood. Although we now know that, no matter how grand the scale of a domestic argument, our blood will only ever boil figuratively, the phrase is still in common usage.

Jailbird
Somebody who has spent time, often repeatedly, in prison. The word is very old, from the sixteenth century, and can be shortened and used to describe serving a prison sentence – 'doing bird'. The image is one of a bird being caged – a free spirit, whose freedom has been curtailed by the jailer.

Jimmy a lock
To jimmy a lock is a phrase used less and less these days, although many people are familiar with it as a term for picking a lock, or breaking it so as to get at whatever the lock is protecting. The word jimmy grew out of jemmy, an English word for the tool used by a robber for

housebreaking. When using a jemmy on a door, one was said to be jemmying. It is widely accepted that jemmy and jimmy derive from the nickname for James, although the identity of the James in question – presumably a master burglar of some kind! – is locked in history and cannot be jimmied out.

John Doe

You would be more likely to hear this term as part of an American detective drama than anything else, where a John Doe is the name given to an unidentified body. In fact, the phrase is an archaic legal term, possibly going back as far as Edward III's reign in the fourteenth century. The names were used to settle land disputes in which an anonymous plaintiff, John Doe, would be evicted by an anonymous defendant, Richard Roe. Why the protagonists' names were rhymed and associated with deer is not known, although this author spuriously speculates that it might have defused a tense atmosphere in the courtroom. John Doe went on to signify an anonymous party in a legal action, or a person whose identity was uncertain.

141

Keep your nose clean

To stay out of trouble. The phrase probably originated in America and was first recorded in 1887. Any parent will know how unsightly the noses of small children can get, and the phrase began as a parental admonishment to get their children to appear smarter. Usage then spilled over into the adult world to talk about things that make adults look smarter – like avoiding petty criminal activity, for example.

Left holding the bag

If you have been left holding the bag, you have, whether you deserve it or not, been given the blame for a situation. The phrase grew out of a similar, yet older, construction – 'giving someone the bag to hold'. This eighteenth-century expression refers figuratively to a situation where a band of criminals on the verge of being caught out would give one of their crew the booty while they made a run for it. Quite obviously, the unfortunate who has been forced to look after the illicit gains has been given the bag to hold, and so takes the blame.

Long arm of the law

The long arm of the law refers light-heartedly to the far-reaching capabilities of the police force who, of course, enforce the law. As an image it is rather cartoon-like, which probably accounts for the fact that it has always been used with a degree of humour or mock-seriousness. It is a nineteenth-century phrase, and borrows from another phrase, 'to make a long arm', which means to reach out as far as possible to pick something up. It is easy to see how the idea works of the police being the figurative long arms that are owned by, and in service of, the law.

Malarkey

Malarkey is a slang term used to mean nonsense or, as the *Oxford English Dictionary* also puts it, 'humbug'. 'What's all this malarkey?' is a common phrase used to express incredulity at a situation. By extension, it can be used to mean 'things in general'. The word is American in origin and dates from the early twentieth century. It is widely reported to have derived from *mullachan*, an Irish word meaning lout or

143

ruffian. Presumably, the slang sense of malarkey derived from an association between louts and nonsensical or pointless things.

On the lam

To be on the lam is to be on the run. 'Lam', 'lammister' and 'on the lam' – all referring to hasty departure – were commonly used slang terms spoken by criminals in the late nineteenth century. The word lam is much older, though, and derives from the Old Norse word for making lame, *lamja*. Since a good way of achieving this is to beat it, it follows that when the word was originally used in Shakespeare's time it meant to beat soundly. (Incidentally, the English word 'lame' grew out of this word too.) The shift in lam's meaning from giving something a good beating to running away from something or someone (that may, indeed, wish to give the escapee a beating) came when another slang term, 'beat it', also meaning to run away, was used as a model for 'lam it'.

Pot

It is thought that this popular nickname for

marijuana comes from a Mexican word *potiguaya*, which means marijuana leaves.

Quango

Quango stands for QUasi Autonomous Non Governmental Organisation. A quango is a shadowy 'non-governmental' body that is funded by the government and whose members are appointed by the government.

Riff-raff

If your parents never told you to not to hang around with riff-raff, perhaps you and yours belonged to this undesirable collective! A dismissive, snooty phrase, it is employed in reference to the perceived lowest common denominator in society, and has become a general term for the unruly, troublemaking and fearsome among us. In short, riff-raff are the unwanted. In medieval times, to rif and raf was to plunder dead bodies (rif) and take off every scrap (raf) of whatever riches were found on them. The phrase had developed from the Old French *rif et raf* meaning 'one and all'. Riff-raff grew from this sense, and an association with persons of low morals and opportunistic instincts existed from the outset. Although today's usage of the word is in no way a reference to thieving soldiers, the flavour of unpleasantness lives on.

Smart alec

A smart alec is someone who is all too keen to show off their knowledge of a subject. Even if the wisdom they might impart is useful, their gloating, smug way of imparting it is unbearably irritating. Your average smart alec knows too much, and will take every opportunity to remind us of this. The term refers to a historical smart alec, one Alex Hoag. Hoag lived in New York in the 1840s and was a notoriously clever and successful thief. Along with his wife Miranda, who was a prostitute, an accomplice named French Jack and two corrupt policemen, Mr Hoag conducted many a petty theft using his beautiful wife to distract his unsuspecting victims while he picked their pockets and handed the loot to French Jack. The police officers were paid to turn a blind eye. A further scam took place whenever Miranda was plying her trade. Her visiting customers, clothes removed, would lie waiting for her. When ready, Miranda would draw a curtain around the bed and once things were in full flow Hoag would enter the room and remove anything of value from the victim's pockets. Then, having quietly left the room, Hoag would turn and knock loudly on the door, pretending to be an angry husband. This, of course, would result in the customer exiting via the window, not noticing what was missing. Eventually Alec Hoag was caught trying to avoid paying off his police officers, and was sentenced to jail. The story goes that the nickname Smart Alec was given to him by the police. After all, they had to acknowledge that, although he was an irritant, he had been pretty clever in what he had done. In this sense, the phrase stuck.

Spiv

A spiv is a slang word for a person who makes a living by underhand dealings, swindling and the black market. The term was at its height in post-Second World War Britain, when a typical spiv would dress expensively, yet tastelessly, and generally show off his mysteriously acquired 'luxury goods'. Speculation is rife about the origin of the word. A common suggestion is that it is VIPs spelled backwards – a spiv is someone who feels themselves to be a VIP (or at least aspires to be seen as such) yet gets it all wrong. This is a possible explanation, but a more likely one is that it is derived from the word spiff, a nineteenth-century word meaning a smartly dressed man about town who, being a snappy dresser, would have been described as spiffy by onlookers.

Time immemorial

Time immemorial is used loosely in the same way as the phrase 'since time began', and also to refer to something that happened so long ago it cannot be remembered. It originates in the thirteenth century when, in 1275, the year 1189 (when Richard I acceded to the throne) was set as being the time beyond which no one could remember. From then on, no legal cases could deal with events before that. The phrase time out of mind, first used in the fifteenth century, is merely the plain-English version of the same thing.

Whistleblower

A government insider, usually pretty close to the top, who exposes the administration's malpractice. The image dates from somewhere in the first half of the twentieth century and is a piece of sporting imagery: the referee blows his whistle to point out a foul and redress the balance of play, which is the same motivation behind so-called whistleblowers inside government organisations.

CHAPTER ELEVEN:
ACROSS THE POND

Paint The Town Red

ACROSS THE POND

Alice blue
A shade of greenish grey-blue that was favoured by Theodore Roosevelt's daughter Alice. The colour became indelibly associated with her name when Harry Tierney wrote the popular song 'Alice Blue Gown', when she was sixteen.

Axe to grind
While the image seems to enforce the idea of someone possessing a kind of edgy bitterness, it actually makes very little sense. However, if you look at it from the point of view of someone who has a hidden agenda, it comes closer to the

original meaning of the expression. The phrase was coined by Benjamin Franklin in an article called 'The Whistle'. In it he describes how he received a visitor who expressed an interest in Franklin's grindstone. Franklin took the axe that the visitor happened to be carrying and proceeded to energetically demonstrate how the grindstone worked using the visitor's axe. Having finished, Franklin realised that he had been duped and that the visitor had intended that Franklin sharpen his axe for him all along. Franklin said that people with an ulterior motive had 'an axe to grind'. Perhaps because of the grim images contained in the expression it has come to be associated with having a more vindictive and sinister ulterior motive.

Buff

A buff is a person whose chosen interest is a serious but amateur pursuit. The word has a bizarre origin. In New York, in the burgeoning days of firefighting (the early 1800s), men would adopt the practice of following fire engines to the scenes of major blazes to watch the firefighters extinguish the flames. There are accounts of such crowds of people cheering the firemen on when they had successes, and groaning when things went wrong. Occasionally they would help the firemen fetch apparatus, although often the firefighters would view such spectators with contempt. During the icy New York winters, they wore buffalo fur to keep warm: the firefighters nicknamed them 'buffalos', which was shortened to 'buffs'.

Bury the hatchet

To bury the hatchet is to make peace with someone by agreeing to forget that which caused or perpetuated a dispute or argument. It originates from the observation of the Native American practice of opposing sides literally burying weapons of war in the ground to mark newly agreed-upon peace. The first hatchet-burying ceremony took place before the arrival of any Europeans, when two Iroquois leaders persuaded the five nations (the Mohawk, Oneida, Onondaga, Cayuga and Seneca) to unify instead of fighting. To acknowledge the newfound peace, the Iroquois buried their weapons under a white pine. The story goes

155

that an underground river washed them away, thus preventing the tribes from using the weapons on each other again. The practice became tradition and, when observed by European missionaries in the seventeenth century, was seized upon as a perfect metaphorical phrase denoting peace-making and problem-solving.

Bushed

To be extremely tired. In Australia, bush remains a term to describe the wilderness, but it was also used by Dutch settlers in the Americas for land that they had cleared of unwanted scrub and trees. Clearing the land was an exhausting activity, and the process of creating habitable land became associated with the effect the intensive labour produced.

For the birds

If something is for the birds, or strictly for the birds, it is a nugget of information or an activity deemed worthless, pointless or just plain impossible. The term did not exist before the twentieth century, and is likely to have originated in the United States. The *Dictionary of Hipster Slang* quotes from *Chicago Chick*, the 1962 novel by Hank Janson ("'It's crazy man," I told him, "real crazy. Strictly for the birds."'). However, it is uncertain whether or not this was the original usage. The phrase is certainly linked with 'bird-brained' though, the idea being that birds have small brains and are therefore stupid. Evidently something that is for the birds is for those humans in possession of far less grey matter than they ought to have.

Gravy train

A gravy train is a well-known metaphor for a source of income that requires little or no effort on the part of the beneficiary. Its origin lies in American slang dating from the early twentieth century, where the word gravy was used to describe something easy to do or resulting from good luck. The idea of a gravy train is suggestive of good luck, or ease, that just keeps on going – not unlike, you may guess, a freight train travelling through the endless American landscape.

Hillbilly

If we call someone a hillbilly, we are probably attempting to insult them, or we are talking behind their back. Now quite a pejorative and dismissive term, it is mostly used by urban dwellers who consider themselves more sophisticated than supposedly less advanced rural hillbillies. A hillbilly venturing into the clutches of the city and its dwellers risks a serious drop in self-esteem by blurting out their ill-conceived, outdated opinions to anyone but themselves – or so we are led to believe. Some of us may associate the term with America, but it is English in origin. Dating from the fifteenth century, the word billy meant a trusted associate or friend. It was a casually affectionate term, a bit like 'chap', 'bloke' or 'fellow'. In the 1800s the word hill merged with it to alter the meaning to one from the country (the 'hills'). It was a matter of time before it was picked up on and used for the purpose of social snobbery, although it can still be used with a degree of affection.

Indian summer

A summer where, after the cold sets in, the

weather suddenly undergoes a miraculous improvement. Things warm up; trees and shrubs get stunned into blooming in November; folk begin muttering about global warming. The Indians in this case are native Americans. There seem to be two theories behind the application of the term. It could be that the summers to the west of the early American settlers were either longer, or the autumn months were prone to lapsing into warmer spells. Or it could be that the word Indian was regrettably being employed euphemistically to denote something that was cheap, in the sense that the Indian summer, being short-lived and unproductive from an agricultural point of view, was useless.

Jaywalk

An American word meaning to cross the road where one is not supposed to. It is a concept that the British have trouble getting to grips with, as crossing the road where you like is not anything unusual in Britain, unless it happens to be motorway. Tradition has it that when the jay bird strayed from its natural habitat, it would often become confused and seem to have a poor sense of where it should put itself. Another theory, and one preferred by the *Oxford English Dictionary*, is that jay was formerly a word meaning a 'silly person' – only silly people, it seems, walk out into the road.

Ku Klux Klan

The name for the unpleasant far-right activists is derived from the Greek word *kuklos* which means circle. The K spelling of 'Klan' is to reinforce the K in 'Ku Klux' for stylistic purposes. How a circle relates to cross-burning and racist lynch mobs is obscure, but a circle can be seen as a symbol of wholeness and purity.

Paint the town red

This phrase, meaning to go out and party in style, originated in the USA in the late 1800s. Etymologists are unsure as to its precise history. One suggested origin is that 'paint' was US slang for 'drink' and that the expression arose out of the fact that, when drunk, a person's face is often reddened. An alternative explanation offers the Wild West as its place of origin. Cowboys in high spirits would drink to excess and express their drunken joy by firing shots into the air and threatening to 'paint the town red' if anyone tried to end their fun. Here, of course, the red is that of blood, but the threats were so empty that the phrase became synonymous with good times and raucous fun.

Play hookey

To play hookey, an American phrase meaning to avoid attendance at school, or play truant, is a phrase whose origins are hard to ascertain. We know that it came about in the mid-nineteenth century, but there are several suggestions as to where it came from. The original 'hooky' (the e was added later) may have arisen out of a splicing of an older phrase 'hook it', which meant to escape or run away from. Of course the t is dropped. It could also be linked to another old word 'hook' meaning to steal – children would 'steal' time off school. The most interesting possibility lies in a comparison between school and fishing where the pain of a child attending school against his or her will is figuratively equated with that of a fish being caught against its will on a hook. Here, playing

161

hookey is associated with 'getting off the hook', or avoiding it in the first place.

Skid row

Skid row is an American term used to describe the poorest, dirtiest part of a town where the dregs of society congregate to drink their lives away in a state of degradation. Its associations are those of failure and desperation, and skid row is seen as the place where people end up when their lives have gone very wrong indeed. Its origin lies in the North American logging industry, where skid row was the row of logs along which other chopped logs rolled, or skidded, during the production process. One town, Tacoma, near Seattle, thrived entirely on timber, and the multitudes of men drawn to the area for the good, steady employment it offered drank as hard as they chopped wood. The vast numbers of lonely workers created a demand for brothels and bars and the place became a magnet for a certain type of man who would fall into these vices. It became a notorious town, and the image contained in the phrase skid row of falling down or slipping meant it passed into the language and became a figurative place where people's lives skid away from them.

Take the cake

A phrase that means to achieve something, but which is generally used ironically, as in, 'My boss was just given a six-figure bonus when I've been doing all his work for him. That really takes the cake!' The expression descends from slavery in the USA. At parties or social gatherings, it was traditional for slaves or free descendants to walk in a procession around a cake until the pair judged to be the most graceful were given a cake as a prize. The phrases 'cake walk' and 'piece of cake', meaning something easily accomplished, sprang from this. It referred to the act of walking around the cake, which, after all, does not sound too difficult.

Teddy bear

The name of this child's toy is also often applied to men who look tough but are 'soft on the inside'. It is language's remarkable achievement to have pacified such a ferocious animal. The

163

history of the teddy bear runs like this. In 1902 Theodore 'Teddy' Roosevelt went to Mississippi to settle a border dispute between Mississippi and Louisiana. To take a break from the negotiations, a hunting trip was organised and, while on this trip, members of the party tied a bear cub to a tree and invited the president to finish the animal off. Roosevelt refused because he felt it was unsporting. The story got out and, the next day, political cartoonist Clifford Berryman drew a worthy Roosevelt refusing to shoot a cute, defenceless bear. The story was charming, and Brooklyn entrepreneur Morris Michtom asked his wife to make two enormous bears for his shop. The bears were adorable, and had black buttons sewn on for eyes. Michtom nicked named them Teddy's Bears. They drew excited enquiries from customers and, in 1906, he went into production of the bears as toys, after securing permission from Roosevelt to do so. However, Michtom's wasn't the only company in the world making stuffed bears. The Steiff jointed bear was being made in Germany at the same time. Their bear was catchily named Bar55PB and apparently had greater emphasis on correct bear anatomy. As the popularity of the teddy bear grew, the Steiff company adopted the term for their animals.

Watergate

A series of complex political scandals that brought down the Nixon administration. Nowadays, if there is some kind of public scandal somewhere, it has become standard practice for journalists to find an aspect of the story and attach the suffix –gate after it. Prince Charles's joke with Camilla that he thought of himself as one of her tampons became Camillagate. On the other side, when Diana, Princess of Wales and James Gilbey were taped repeating the pet names they had for each other down the phone, the affair became Squidgygate. When it was revealed that Cherie Blair had a dubious association with con man Peter Foster, we all read about Cheriegate. The original scandal that has allowed journalists to come up with a handy catch-all term for whatever outrage comes along next is really the greatest of all modern political scandals as it revealed breathtaking corruption in the world's most powerful government, and led to the resignation of the president of the world's most powerful nation. In 1973 two journalists, Carl Bernstein and Bob Woodward, were given a tip-off by an anonymous source whom they named Deep Throat. Deep Throat revealed that, during the 1972 presidential election, the Republican party had bugged the Democrat offices next to the river Potomac in Washington known as Watergate. A scandal erupted and senior Whitehouse officials were prosecuted. The trail seemed to lead all the way to the top and President Richard Nixon resigned rather than face impeachment. In 2005, FBI man Mark Felt revealed that he was Deep Throat.

Whippersnapper

An overconfident youngster, or baby or small child with an exceptional amount of energy. Nowadays the word is employed quite affectionately. However, like every generation, doubtless from the time of Adam, there reaches a stage in the development of a young male when, if he can, he will employ his days in needless sensationalism. In the wasted west of

America a couple of centuries back, practising snapping a whip on the corner did the trick. On my street, as the evenings draw in every year, it appears to be chucking fireworks ...

Whistle-stop tour

When we talk of a whistle-stop tour, we are usually referring to a travel experience that takes in many different places quickly over a reasonably short period of time. The term whistle-station has its roots in the interwar United States. Often, trains would not stop at small towns unless requested to do so by a passenger. When such a request was made, the driver would sound the train's whistle twice to indicate the train would pull in at the next stop. So the term came to refer to small places that many would not have heard of. The sense of a whistle-stop tour meaning a speedy political campaign developed when President Truman embarked upon his 1948 election campaign by train, delivering speech after speech in several different locations every day. In Los Angeles, the president jokingly referred to the fact that the city was the biggest whistle-stop he had visited. The crowd roared its approval, but he had slipped up – the correct term was whistle-station. In making his error, Harry Truman coined a phrase that stuck. We still use it in a political context, but also in reference to our own adventures.

Whole kaboodle

The term the whole kaboodle, or the whole kit and kaboodle, is tantamount to saying 'the lot' or 'the whole lot'. The phrase developed from the use of 'the whole boodle' in early nineteenth-century America, 'boodle' meaning ill-gotten money acquired through bribery and laundering. This sense has not been lost, as today we often use the whole kaboodle in reference to objects or situations of questionable legitimacy. Kit, perhaps obviously, refers to equipment, so we can see that the whole kit and kaboodle signifies all that a person has, and perhaps all they need.

CHAPTER TWELVE:
FALSE FRIENDS

Brand Spanking New

FALSE FRIENDS

Barking mad

Barking mad may seem self-evident in its meaning. We assume that someone who is barking mad is labelled so owing to their being so strange that they bear an uncanny resemblance to a mad dog. While this works as an explanation, there is a strong possibility that the phrase actually originated from a medieval lunatic asylum located in Barking, London. The asylum was notorious for its extremely troubled residents, and the term caught on as a label for anyone who behaved as if they would not be out of place in the institution.

Bated breath

To wait with bated breath is to be in a state of anxiety and fear, or to be expecting an answer to or explanation of something. The word bate dates from the 1300s, and bated breath appears in Shakespeare's *The Merchant of Venice*: 'Shall I bend low and, in a bondman's key, With bated breath and whisp'ring humbleness, Say this …' There is sometimes confusion as to whether it should be spelled bated or baited. In fact, 'baited breath' is merely a modern corruption of the phrase – people mistakenly understand the breath to be baited like a hook or trap, metaphorically poised to catch something. It works in a way, but it is not the real McCoy. The original form of the phrase is much more literal – bate is another word for abate, meaning to cut short, hold back or suspend. Hence bated breath is a sharp intake of breath, or breath being held, momentarily ceased with expectancy.

Black box

An aircraft's flight recorder. Black boxes are, in fact, bright orange, so that they can be better seen by recovery crews. They are nicknamed 'black' because the data in them is unknown and, until the box is recovered, mysterious. An Australian chemist, Dr David Warren, came up with the idea in 1954, but it wasn't until a decade later that their use became widespread.

Brand spanking new

We use the phrase brand spanking new to refer to something that's, well, *very* new! A common explanation of its origin is that of it having referred to a newly born child needing to be spanked in order to help it begin breathing. Thus, the phrase works as a peculiar sort of comparison: anything brand spanking new – a pair of jeans, perhaps – is as new and fresh (and wonderful) as a baby. Cute, but wrong. First found in the sixteenth century, the original sense of brand new comes from the marks made by a hot iron on cattle – a brand. It later came to be associated with an identifying mark of any sort. It is easy to see how this transfers to our modern understanding of brands and products. 'Spanking', which elbows itself in between the words of an already complete phrase to form a more emphatic one, popped up in English during the seventeenth century to indicate an especially fine quality in something. After then being applied to describe exceptionally good, fast horses, its meaning widened to mean any speedy movement. For the purposes of this phrase though, which was first used in the nineteenth century, it is only the first sense of spanking, meaning something fine and remarkable, that works.

Chav

A chav is a sneery term for someone with exceptionally (there's just no avoiding this word) *common* taste; a chav, like a chinless wonder, is unlikely to have an IQ in triple digits – like kids in Burberry hats and, well, Victoria and David Beckham. But where did this modern word come from? Council House And Violent? CHeltenham AVerage? As a broad rule, if any explanation is as easy and as neat as that, it's a false friend. Chav is from the gypsy language Romany. The Romany word for boy, *chavi*, and man, *chava*, have been appropriated, because of their gypsy origins, to become an insult.

Cheap at half the price

People freely use the expression cheap at half the price, but intriguingly it can have totally opposing meanings depending on the intentions of whoever is using it! Some resort to it in order to say that they've found something to be a bargain, others will use it to indicate that they think something is a rip-off. The question is, which usage is correct? To find out, we need to examine the literal meaning of the phrase. If a monkey is for sale at £1,000 and we comment that it would be cheap at half the price, surely we mean that the monkey is either fairly priced or expensive. After all, if the monkey were already considered cheap, then it would be even cheaper at half the price, not merely cheap. To indicate that something is a bargain, the construction cheap at *twice* the price would make much more sense. Looking at it in these terms, it is surely correct to assume that cheap at half the price works best as a sarcastic comment to indicate that something that a shop, for instance, is claiming to be incredible value is in fact rather the opposite. If we punctuate the phrase to say something is 'cheap, at half the price', we may conclude that it simply means it is being sold at a discount and has become cheap. Either way, the phrase endures in all its mind-boggling ambiguity. And no, the author does not own a monkey.

Crap

There is a common misconception that Thomas Crapper lent his name to this word, which describes a human stool and the action of producing such a specimen. However, while Thomas Crapper was indeed in the toilet trade, he didn't invent the flushing toilet and the word crap was around before he was born. Its origin is in the Latin *crappa*. In Old French and Middle English the word became *crappe*, which described the grain in a barn that was trodden underfoot. The word became shortened over time, and its association with waste products ideally placed it to take up the dubious honour of representing faecal matter, as well as poorly chosen words.

Exception that proves the rule

The exception that proves the rule is a classic

phrase that continues to be misunderstood and discussed from one generation to the next. We normally use it to indicate that something is out of the ordinary, although to imagine that an exception can mean that a rule is true does seem to be nonsensical – after all, an exception indicates the rule doesn't work. The reason that the phrase seems so paradoxical is that, when thinking about its meaning, we all focus on an incorrect meaning of the word exception. The word exception derives from the Latin *exceptio*, which originally meant something that is permitted *not* to follow a rule or law. To illustrate, imagine a situation where a mother says to her children, 'You may have ice cream on Fridays.' From this, we (and the kids, it is hoped) can infer that they are not allowed ice cream on any other day. So, quite simply, the exception that proves the rule is really an allowed or confirmed and pre-arranged exception that implicitly draws attention to the existence of a rule.

Head over heels

Being head over heels is almost always to be in love. Those who are in such a state are usually in the early stages of romance where all cares, responsibilities and other friends are forgotten and the happy couple are deliriously obsessed with each other to the point that their worlds (figuratively at least) have been turned upside down and everything seems rather fresh, new and exciting. Charming stuff indeed, but why head over heels when, literally speaking, we are always in this position? Surely heels over head would make more sense as an expression of change and newness, of 'upsidedownness'. Well, originally, that was indeed the expression, which quite obviously meant to be performing a somersault. The phrase heels over head was itself turned upside down by Davy Crockett, the most famous man to ever wear a racoon on his head, when he described being in love with a certain young lady. From the early nineteenth century this new version, or *in*version, of the expression stuck, despite its questionable logic.

Hooker

A prostitute. It is often mistakenly believed that this word originates from the once legendary exploits of Joseph 'Fighting Jo' Hooker, a

general in the American Civil War. It was said
that the general was 'a man of blemished
character whose headquarters was a place no
self-respecting man liked to go and no decent
woman could go'. It seems that the general
assembled a great many prostitutes in an area
that became known as 'Hooker's Division' in
Washington around 1850. However, the word
actually dates from before this time, and the
general's antics probably did no more than
reinforce what was already widely used. The
exact origin is uncertain. It may have come from
an area of Manhattan known as Corlear's Hook
where prostitutes plied their trade. It may also
have come from the Dutch slang word *huckster*,
which means 'someone who entices'.

Keep mum

The phrase keep mum has nothing at all to do
with mothers. As many will know, to keep mum
is to decide to keep quiet, keep one's mouth shut
and not say a word – in short, it is to keep a
secret. Its origin is delightfully simple. Mum is
merely the spelling chosen to represent the only
sound it is possible for a person to make if their

mouth is tightly shut – the unintelligible 'Mmmm'. It has been around in various forms for over 500 years and its meaning has not changed. It is worth pointing out that the sense of mum referring to a mother, or mummy, did not exist until the nineteenth century, so until then the phrase could never have been used with any double meaning or irony.

Posh

The theory behind this word that is most often quoted is that it is an acronym for Port Out Starboard Home. It is supposed to refer to passenger ships steaming their way to and from India. The best cabins would be on the shady side of the ship when cruising through tropical seas. This would be on the left side going out from Britain and the right side on the way back. The tickets of the rich would therefore be marked P.O.S.H., in order to ensure that they were given the correct cabins. There has been extensive research into this theory, apparently, and no tickets with the acronym have been found, despite the fact that there are plenty of tickets from the era still in existence. It certainly isn't true. There is a theory that it does come, in a very roundabout way, from India, but via Romany gypsies. They had their roots in the north of India, as does the language itself, which is based on the ancient tongue Sanskrit. Posh means half in Romany and half pennies were commonly called *posh-houri*. The phrase became common parlance when referring to money in general, and by extension those who had plenty of it. If you do accept this theory, it is perhaps interesting to reflect how 'posh' has become a qualitative term rather than just a quantitative one about money, and to use the word now is to engage with the myriad complexities of the British class system. It's not just about cash.

Stick in the mud

A stick in the mud is a consummate bore, a character whose views are conservative, whose behaviour is as daring and flamboyant as watching the snooker, someone whose ways are unlikely to change. Some say that the expression finds its origin in pirate law whereby, if on land and therefore unable to walk the plank, a mutinous crew member would be buried up to his neck in the sand, or mud, at low tide. There is little evidence that this practice ever existed, but it makes a good story. The idea of a person being literally stuck does tally with the notion of a bore who is stuck in his ways, figuratively immovable, so there is some sense in it. However, there is a more likely explanation, which points out that the phrase, dating from the mid-eighteenth century, probably grew out of 'stick in the mire', used to describe someone who is dull, stubborn, uncreative and complacent.

CHAPTER THIRTEEN:
LOST IN
TRANSLATION

Black Market

LOST IN TRANLATION

Black market

We use this term to describe any illegal trade whereby goods and services are bought and sold at cheaper prices than in legitimate outlets, and also to refer to currency-dealing where black-market exchange rates differ from official ones. A popular explanation of its origin is that it initially referred to the sale of 'fire-damaged' goods (ie goods that were said to have been lost in a fire, but had actually been 'salvaged' or stolen), although there is not enough evidence to be sure of this. What can be confirmed is that the English phrase is a direct translation of the

German *Schwarzmarkt*, and was adopted by soldiers during the First World War. It became a standard phrase during the Second World War, and referred to not only the trade in stolen military supplies (clothing, blankets, food and the like), but also the domestic buying and selling of rationed goods. After the war, it endured as a general term for illicit dealings.

Blue blood

The term blue blood has been widely used in Britain since the nineteenth century to refer to a member of the aristocracy. It comes directly from the Spanish *sangre azul*, meaning, well, blue blood! Families from Castile were very keen to stress their difference from the Moors, who had controlled Spain for years. To prove their breeding, they claimed that their veins were a purer blue than those of inferior, foreign origin. The reason for this, of course, was because their blue blood could be seen through their white skin; the Moors had dark skin, so their veins could not be seen. The term was appropriated by English aristocratic families during the nineteenth century, when it was a mark of deep

186

social inferiority to have a suntan. To start with, to be tanned meant that you had spent the days outdoors, *working* for a living. These days we work indoors, so a tan shows that you get out more and have leisure and money to fly to foreign climes and sit about in the sun. Formerly, however, if you had visible blue veins showing, you had blue blood and would be praised accordingly.

Bonzer

A stereotypical Australian exclamation, used as a positive affirmation of a situation – you say it when things are going well, much as you would say 'Great!', 'Super!' or 'Fantastic!' Less in use in its country of origin than British comedians would have us believe, the origin of the word is probably a combination of *bon*, the French word for good, and *bonanza*, a Spanish word meaning fair weather.

Brouhaha

A tremendous word meaning, according the *Oxford English Dictionary*, 'commotion, sensation, hubbub, uproar'. Brouhaha was borrowed in the nineteenth century directly from the identical French. Before then, it often appeared in sixteenth-century French dramas as the Devil's cry, announcing his arrival in scenes. It is commonly accepted that brouhaha derives from the Hebrew for 'welcome', *barukh habba*, used at Jewish celebrations. The link between the Jewish sense 'welcome' and commotion and uproar is easy to make – hubbub and sensation are, after all, common at any good party! A reasonable explanation of the choice of brouhaha as the Devil's cry is that it was an act of anti-Semitism, all too common at the time.

Cockles of the heart

Flowers, weddings and presents beneath the tree on Christmas day all warm the cockles of your heart. While the term heart-warming is well understood, however, it is less well known why the heart's cockles need warming, or even where they are. It seems most likely that the expression comes from a corruption of the Latin *cochleae cordis*, which refers to what we now call the ventricles of the heart. The ventricles are the chambers that pump blood around the body.

There is another theory that the heart's ventricles resemble a cockle; whether this is true or not, it certainly reinforces the expression's usage.

Coin a phrase

To make a new expression. The phrase is perhaps a little less unusual if you consider that *coinen*, in Middle English, meant to mint money. To coin a phrase, therefore, is to mint a new phrase.

Foolscap

A size of paper. The word originally comes from the Italian *foglio-capo* which means 'folio sized'. Folios of paper were folded in half to form two leaves of a book. Foolscap is now the standard paper size for typed documents in America, wider than the A4 that is common to the UK. The *Oxford English Dictionary* suggests an alternative theory, which is that early foolscap sheets contained a watermark with an image of a fool's cap.

Gibberish

One of the common explanations given for the origin of 'gibberish' is that it has its basis in the old word 'gibber', which in turn is connected to 'jabbering', and therefore nonsense. It is a convenient explanation, but as 'gibberish' was in use before 'gibber', it is itself gibberish. The true origin of the word is found in the name of an eleventh-century Arabian alchemist, Geber, who invented bizarre and coded terminology in order to hide the meaning of his work from others. This allowed his techniques to remain a secret and, moreover, protected him from charges of heresy, which was punishable by death. Gibberish developed from this sense of encoded meaning to be used in a derogatory manner. If we accuse a partner, lover, business partner or child of talking gibberish, we are accusing them of speaking incomprehensible nonsense, although the connection with the past can be seen, as what the patient listener perceives to be utter rubbish may indeed mean something to the speaker. The modern sense came into use in the early 1800s.

Gingerly

If we do something gingerly, we do not perform

our task accompanied by a piece of the fiery root – unless, of course, we are gingerly peeling some ginger, which seems unlikely, or gingerly approaching an intimidating-looking purveyor of the spice to make a nervous purchase. Ginger has nothing to do with the origin of the word gingerly, a pretty little adverb meaning cautiously, reluctantly or timidly. It derives from the Old French word *genzor*, the comparative form of *gent*, meaning 'delicate'. To see the connection between delicate action and caution is to understand how the term evolved.

Hoo-ha

'What a hoo-ha!' we might exclaim, exasperated by a scene of uproar or witnessing a fiery argument between an animated group of people. It is a twentieth-century phrase for a commotion of any kind, and originates from the Yiddish *hu-ha*, which means the same thing.

Hullabaloo

Hullabaloo, like hoo-ha, is a wonderfully effective word to sum up a situation of clamour, uproar and general commotion. Although it sounds rather like a nonsense word that is resonant of fuss and mayhem, both in its spelling and pronunciation, its origin lies in the French *hurluberlu*, a seventeenth-century word meaning scatter-brained. It is easy to see how the sense of chaos is present in this meaning, as it is in the English derivative.

Jeopardy
To be in jeopardy is to be in danger of injury, loss or death and so on. It derives directly from the French *jeu parti*, meaning 'divided game' and therefore of uncertain, dangerous, outcome.

Kerfuffle
A kerfuffle is a commotion or fuss, and is often used to describe a situation where confusion has taken over. It is originally a Scottish word, with the ker part deriving from *car*, the Gaelic for to bend or twist. The second part, fuffle, is a Scots dialect word meaning to ruffle or cause disorder. The word fuff meant to give out puffs of smoke, and these different elements of meaning (all with connotations of confusion and mess)

combined with the oddly pleasing sound of the word meant that kerfuffle became, by the beginning of the twentieth century, a word that made no obvious sense to most but which nevertheless served to describe all manner of strange situations.

Loo

Although we know the word loo originates from the French, we cannot be sure what French it is derived from, and exactly how it came to mean toilet is a bit of a mystery! The most endearing origin, and one that is entirely plausible, is that in times before anything faintly resembling what we now understand to be a loo, housewives and maids would precede emptying their chamber pots out of the window on to the street by shouting 'Gardey loo!', a corruption of the French *gardez l'eau* – 'mind the water'. Another possibility is that it is a euphemism for toilet derived from the French *le lieu*, meaning 'the place' (*lieu* is pronounced similarly to loo). A third option is that the French *lieu d'aisance*, meaning 'place of ease', was adopted by British soldiers in the First World War and used as a polite substitute for toilet. Whatever the truth is about the origin of loo, all three possibilities contain within them the desire to be euphemistic – after all, what goes into a loo is more than *l'eau*, the place is hardly a desirable place to be and it is not always a place of ease!

Nightmare

The term derives from Old English and from the word *maere*, an evil fiend. Night *maeres* would stalk about at night, causing wickedness and ill will. It was also assumed that they were the cause of terrifying dreams.

Pardon my French

Excuse my bad language. France has often been on the receiving end of the UK's taboos. The associating of the French language with things the British have regarded as obscene can also be found in such phrases as 'French letter' for condom and 'French kiss' for a snog. The French came in for another recent linguistic bashing when moves were made in United States government cafeterias to rechristen 'French fries' and 'French toast' as 'freedom fries' and 'freedom toast' because of a disagreement on foreign policy between the two nations.

Pidgin English

Pidgin English is thought to have originated in China after the British established a trading post in Canton in 1664. However, Portugal established trade in China before the British, so Portuguese is an often neglected influence on pidgin English. Pidgin English didn't fully emerge until the end of the seventeenth century. It was developed as a way of accommodating the speakers of two very different languages so that they could do business with each other. So, 'pidgin English' really means 'business English', and 'pidgin' is thought to be a mispronunciation of the English word 'business' by the Chinese. The pidgin that was originally spoken in China contained aspects of both Cantonese and English, and was spoken as a second language by both English traders and the indigenous Chinese traders. In the last century, the language became more anglicised.

Swag

Swag means different things to different people. It can refer to a robber's booty, free products, a prize giveaway or the sum of a traveller's – or swagman's – worldly goods. Whether or not we use it to mean 'hot' property or giveaways, it always refers to something that has been gained freely. The word is Scandinavian in origin, from *swagga*, meaning 'to hang loosely'. From our childhoods we are all familiar with the image of a sagging bag on the end of a stick containing swag – the interesting thing is that, at the beginning of the nineteenth century, swag referred to the bag containing stolen goods, not the goods themselves. By the mid-nineteenth century, the term was used to refer to the items.

CHAPTER FOURTEEN:
ARTS AND ENTERTAINMENT

Pipe Dream

ARTS AND ENTERTAINMENT

Barnstorming

American actors travelled from town to town in the nineteenth century and would give performances anywhere that offered them a makeshift stage. More often than not, a suitably large sheltered venue would turn out to be a farmer's barn. A barnstorming performance was literally one that created a sensation in the barn. Borrowing a perceived notion of what these performances must have been like, we now apply the word to a performance (usually by a politician) that has a kind of powerful, *ad hoc* immediacy to it.

Bowdlerise

To bowdlerise is to censor something and weed out any profane or sexual language, and is usually meant negatively. The word is a tribute to Thomas Bowdler who published *The Family Shakespeare* in 1818. Bowdler was irked that a man could not read Shakespeare aloud to his family without running into the strong language and bawdy puns that litter the bard's work. He went through the complete works and, through sly paraphrase and not so sly word substitution, produced an edition of twenty plays that were suitable for children. Rumour has it that much of the work, if not all, was down to his spinster sister Harriet. Of course, Harriet, being a spinster, did not want it going around that she actually knew what any of the colourful language meant, so she was quite content not to appear alongside her brother's name.

Claptrap

Nowadays, claptrap is mindless rubbish, but it is originally a theatrical term from the eighteenth century. It described a speech or scene that was contrived to elicit a favourable response from an audience – a trap to make you clap. It wouldn't necessarily be totally off the plot, but it would stand out as a set piece.

Cut to the chase
To come to the point. The term comes to us from the cinema. It describes the moment when the film moves from a slower piece of action to a more stimulating scene, usually a car chase.

Disco
The word disco is French in origin, coming from *discothèque*, which means 'record library'. The first discothèques played jazz in secret clubs in Paris during the Second World War. The inhabitants of Nazi-occupied Paris couldn't risk being caught listening to live jazz bands, so records were used in their place. After the war, events at which records were the focal point of the evening became more popular, but the word *discothèque* didn't really go global until the seventies. Discothèques became associated with venues that played a particular kind of funky dance music, which became known as disco.

Double whammy

A twofold setback or unpleasant blow. A whammy is an American word for a hex or curse. It was first recorded in the 1920s, but probably existed before then. It is onomatopoeic, coming from 'wham' – a word that was no doubt considered to aptly describe the impact of an evil curse. The double whammy is thought to be the creation of the cartoonist Al Capp in his comic *Li'l Abner*. A character from the strip, Evil-Eye Fleegle, had the power to paralyse opponents with his gaze. Directing just one eye, a single whammy, was apparently pretty devastating; the double whammy – a two-eyed stare – was lethal.

Funk

Funk once meant a smell. It was used to describe the foggy fug created by many smokers gathered together in a room, and we can well imagine that alcohol fumes were often added to the mix. It is not known exactly how it mutated into meaning a particular kind of rhythmic music, but there are two main theories. The first is to do with the odour surrounding the music –

the smoky 'funk' of a club or the odour of a musician after they have played a particularly hard session. There is also the theory that funk is, in fact, the sexual odour of an aroused woman, perhaps caused by the excitement of listening to funky music.

Geek

Geek isn't quite the insult it used to be. The initial enthusiasm for owning a new household appliance like, say, a toaster can in these troubled times give way to helpless anger once the thing is actually plugged in and won't do anything other than sit there winking cryptically at you. So, as computers take over and familiar objects come to resemble props from *Star Trek*, the geek has become synonymous with knowing how these things work. With this comes restored status ... and even riches. Your original geek was emphatically not in away laudable, and was vastly more unhealthy and unattractive than the modern version. He was a performer in a carnival or circus show whose function was to be depraved and disgusting. He would do things like bite the heads off chickens and other small animals, and the crowd would be appalled, revolted and thrilled. The word possibly comes from the old Scottish *geck*, which means fool. So this performer was a contemptible oddball on the margins of fairground culture, which was itself on the margins of society. Bullies, being what they are, naturally employed this name to insult the class misfit and, of course, the class misfit is so often the only one doing the work. Nowadays, of course, the geeks shall inherit the earth.

Goody Two Shoes

Somebody who is very, perhaps nauseatingly, well behaved. Goody Two Shoes was actually a character in an early children's book. John Newbury is widely recognised as one of the first and perhaps the greatest children's publisher. He only published writers of the highest calibre, and Oliver Goldsmith, author of the eighteenth-century West End triumph *She Stoops to Conquer*, is alleged to have written the story that gave rise to this phrase. It appeared in 1765 and involved a virtuous pauper who wanders the streets of London with only one shoe on. Eventually she is awarded for her down-the-line antics and is given a new pair of shiny shoes. Delighted by the gift, she shows her joy by exclaiming, 'Two shoes! Two shoes!' As the story progresses, more gifts are showered upon her and, in the manner of all good pre-modernist narratives, Miss Goody Two Shoes winds up at the end of a story with a fortune.

Green room
An area where performers can relax when they are not on stage. Green rooms are found in theatres and even television studios everywhere, and they needn't necessarily be painted green. The first green rooms were in London theatres in the early eighteenth century, and it is most likely that they were so named because they tended to be painted a pale green to soothe the actors and calm them down before and in between appearing on stage.

Hip
To be cool. But to be hip, you need to be up on fringe knowledge as well. Hipsters lead where

the cool can only follow. The original use of this word is not clear. Some say it refers to modes of holding a saxophone, holding the bell of the instrument close to the hip (like Lester Young), or 'square' with the instrument held rigidly parallel to the body (like John Coltrane). But surely Coltrane was pretty hip himself, so that wouldn't explain why square means not cool. One thing's for sure, and that is that the word's origins begin in African-American culture. According to *Brewer's Dictionary* hip was from the west African language Wolof, where *hipi* means 'to open one's eyes' and a *hipi-kat* was one who had opened their eyes. A hepcat in 1950s beat jargon was a scenester who loved loud music and dancing, and who had opened their eyes to the enlightened jazz scene. Hip became a term synonymous with those who were 'turned on' to modern culture and, despite fluctuations in popularity, it's a word that is still fairly common today.

Hocus-pocus

Meaningless babble designed to conceal the truth. Hocus Pocus was a magician who performed his tricks for James I. He derived his name from his full incantation, which he used to dazzle and distract his audience while he performed his trick: 'Hocus Pocus, tontus talontus, vade celeriter jubeo!' This is Latin-sounding nonsense but, as his fame attests, it must have done the trick.

Jolly D
A cheery – and now rather quaint – affirmation that all is well. It became the catchphrase of actor Maurice Denham's hapless character Dudley Davenport in the humorous radio programme *Much Binding in the Marsh*. Jolly D stands for 'jolly decent'.

Jolly hockey sticks
Jolly hockey sticks is a very English phrase, used to parody and mock a certain class of girl or woman in Britain. Hockey is a game that was originally played mostly by privileged girls from rich families who attended fee-paying public schools, and it became associated with the rather gung-ho, rustically carefree and wholesomely sporting attitude of the schools

and those who attended them. In the 1950s the phrase was born out of an incredibly popular BBC radio comedy show named *Educating Archie*, which included a character called Monica, played by Beryl Reid, who parodied the archetypal girl's public school pupil displaying all the characteristics of blinkered privilege and the cheery ignorance that can results from her position in life. The phrase caught the public's imagination as an image perfectly suited to sum up a certain stereotype. We may call someone 'a bit jolly hockey sticks' to indicate, with only very mild nastiness, that they are of a type whom we consider different to, and somewhat less down to earth from, ourselves.

Mission impossible

Mission impossible is a commonly used phrase employed lightly to describe frustrating situations or seemingly impossible tasks, like not being able to fix a washing machine, or trying to get through to your boss. The term sprung from the American TV spy thriller series *Mission: Impossible*, broadcast between 1966 and 1973 and originally starring Steven Hill.

Mojo

Mike Myers gave the word mojo a resurgence in the film *Austin Powers*. By the time Myers got to it, he chose to use it euphemistically with reference to Austin Powers's apparently protean sex drive and the instrument used to administer it. However, the word, while usually associated with sex, really has its roots in African magic and possibly in the Gullah language that came into being on the west coast of Africa – the slave coast – around the eighteenth century. The word *moco* in Gullah meant magic or witchcraft. The word mojo surfaced in numerous blues tunes and referred to a magic charm or amulet, as well as magic itself. The magic or amulet is often described snaring men and women sexually. Jim Morrison sang about Mr Mojo Risin' in 'LA Woman'. Mr Mojo Risin' is an anagram of Jim Morrison.

Nitty-gritty

Nitty-gritty is used to describe the key issues, essentials or the basis of a problem or situation, and most often arises in the phrase 'get down to the nitty-gritty'. In 1963 it entered into popular speech in America following the release of a song entitled 'The Nitty Gritty', sung by Shirley Ellis. The record contains the line 'Now let's get right on down to the nitty-gritty'. Nitty-gritty refers to the small grit-like nits or lice that are difficult to get out of one's hair or scalp. The analogy is that the essentials of a problem are often hard to separate from other factors.

Pipe dream
This phrase, describing a plan or scheme that will never happen, has its roots in the eighteenth century. The pipe in this case is an opium pipe, and the ideas and the thoughts and theories that one has after smoking the pipe are of course narcotically inspired and so are able to sidestep rational and practical confines.

Pleased as Punch
To be extremely pleased, bordering on the smug. This homely saying has in its roots more sinister undertones than you would first expect. Punch refers to the sadistic Mr Punch who, as many a child has discovered, is a rather aggressive individual. He murders his baby, is

210

caught by his wife (whom he then beats to death) and is jailed. He escapes and proceeds to kill, among others, a policeman, a judge and the Devil himself. The quintessentially English character of Mr Punch actually originated in medieval Italian theatre. He was imported through travelling theatre and became a popular fixture in the plays performed in English summer carnivals. A key theme of these carnivals was an inversion of the usual social order, and so the psychopathic Mr Punch, who beats his wife, the law and Satan, might well be pleased.

CHAPTER FIFTEEN:
RELIGION

Escape By The Skin of Your Teeth

RELIGION

Doubting Thomas
Somebody who is sceptical or dubious that an event will occur. One of Jesus's twelve disciples, Thomas was doubtful of the resurrection, even after Jesus had appeared and spoken to them. In order to verify that it was indeed Christ before him, Jesus let Thomas feel the wound in his side that had been created by the Roman soldier who wounded him on the cross: 'Then saith he to Thomas, reach hither thy finger, and behold my hands, and reach hither thy hand, and thrust it into my side: and be not faithless, but believing' (John 20:27). Some claim that this

was written by John to undermine *The Gospel of St Thomas*, discovered in Egypt in 1946. Thomas's portrayal of Jesus is different in character to John's. In Thomas's gospel, Jesus preaches self-enlightenment over worship of God alone. If you accept this side of the story then the phrase doubting Thomas is a piece of biblical propaganda that continued to survive well after Thomas's teachings had been lost from any kind of mainstream Christian teaching.

Escape by the skin of your teeth

To have a very narrow escape. This strange image comes from the Bible, specifically the story of the beleaguered Job who is the victim of an awesome cosmic bet between God and Satan. Satan bets God that he can get Job to curse God's name. God agrees to the bet, giving Satan carte blanche to do his worst. Satan tortures Job by covering him from head to foot with excruciating boils. In his pain, poor old Job declares at one point, 'My bone cleaveth to my skin and to my flesh, and I am escaped with the skin of my teeth' (Job 19: 20). Perhaps the pain had left him demented and unable to think straight. Perhaps the skin on his face was eroded to the gums. The situation is clear, though – Job's escape was exceedingly narrow. We now escape 'by' (rather than 'with') the skin of our teeth. Whether the actual 'skin' of the teeth is the enamel or the gums is something we'll probably never be sure of.

For Pete's sake

This commonly used euphemism for 'for God's sake' has been in use since around the beginning of the twentieth century. The choice of the name Pete is an abbreviation of St Peter, and we use the phrase when something or someone is disappointing us. It is perfect as an expression of irritation, guaranteed not to offend yet strangely satisfying either to mutter under the breath or scream from the rafters.

In the biblical sense

This phrase can be used literally to make clear that a word in modern usage should be interpreted as it would be understood by readers of the Bible (for example, the words swear, spirit and father can have entirely different meanings depending on their usage). But these days, to use the phrase 'in the biblical sense' and not expect a laugh is unusual: it is more often than not bound up with the sexual connotations of a word or phrase. To 'know someone' in the biblical sense is the most often used example. Based on the use of the verb 'to know' in the King James Bible (as in 'And Adam knew Eve his wife; and she conceived, and bare Cain, and said, I have gotten a man from the Lord' (Genesis 4:1)) is to be more than merely acquainted with them – it is to be sexually intimate with them. In this context, the phrase is most often used humorously and euphemistically.

Jesus H Christ!

This is a spin on 'Jesus Christ!' or 'Jesus!' as an oath. The H variety is mostly used to emphasise an exasperation or disbelief, and is effected with heavy emphasis on the H. Its origins are American and it has been in use since the 1800s. The expression itself comes from Greek. IHΣ (iota, eta, sigma) is a monogram made from the first two letters of Jesus's name in Greek, with the last letter tacked on at the end. The H, although the Greek capital letter for eta, was at some point mistaken for the Latin H, and the phrase as we know it grew out of this.

Kiss of death

An action or event that will lead to certain failure. The original kiss of death was the kiss given by Judas to Jesus. When Judas decided to betray Jesus to the Romans, he told them that he would identify Jesus by giving him a kiss on the cheek. It was this kiss that resulted in his being tried and nailed to the cross. Mafia bosses in Sicily are said to have taken a shine to Judas's way of doing things and, in a custom called *omerta*, a mobster would receive a kiss from the boss shortly before being 'dealt with'.

Knock on wood

Knock on wood is often casually used when people want to give themselves some luck. The wood in the phrase alludes to Jesus's crucifixion, and the superstition is rooted in Christian folklore.

Once in a blue moon

Something that happens once in a blue moon is something that happens very rarely. Strangely enough, this does not actually refer to a freak event – astronomically speaking, blue moons roll round about every one and a half years, and are actually nothing more than the occurrence of two full moons in a calendar month. When the modern western calendar was set up, it was anchored firmly to the Church calendar and the idea that there are twelve moons every year. The date of Easter is decided according to the appearance of the full moon.[1] When a second moon occurred in the month, it was termed a 'blue moon', as opposed to an ecclesiastical full moon. So, while a blue moon may be a rare event, strictly speaking it isn't one that will never happen.

Protestant

The Protestant branch of Christianity dates from a meeting at Spire in Germany in 1529

---

1 The full explanation of when Easter must fall is this: Easter Sunday is the first Sunday following the first full moon that occurs on or after the day of the vernal equinox.

(known as the Diet of Spires). Those present signed a protestation against a papal decree banning the teachings of Martin Luther. Dissenting Christians became collectively know as Protestants – protestors. Martin Luther saw the Catholic Church as having strayed from the original teachings of the Bible and corrupted by self-interested clerics who used papal authority to seek political advantage rather than pursue God's work.

Red letter day
A day of exceptional good fortune or celebration. In the *Book of Common Prayer*, first issued in 1549, important Christian festivals such as Christmas, Easter and saints' days were marked in red ink. These days were also marked in red on calendars.

Tub-thumping
If a person is tub-thumping, or a tub-thumper, they deliver their (perhaps unwanted) opinions with a forceful and clumsy expansiveness. This loud form of rhetoric is designed to linguistically bludgeon an audience into

submission and agreement. The term originally referred to a preacher or orator who banged on a pulpit or table while speaking. Often, when outside, a speaker would use an actual tub as a substitute for a lectern. This honourable tradition is today maintained in religion and politics, only without the tubs.

Zounds!

An ancient oath, now sadly archaic – although it does crop up in a number of Shakespeare's plays. The word derives from an old oath, 'Christ's wounds!', slurred together so that it loses its profanity.

CHAPTER SIXTEEN:
AT WORK

Fly Off The Handle

AT WORK

Chip off the old block

This phrase has its origins in images of carpentry and, today, is almost exclusively used to suggest that aspects of a son's characteristics, be they physical or behavioural, bear a strong similarity to those of his father. The phrase, originally chip of the same block, was used from the sixteenth century to refer to either child in reference to either parent. A perfect little metaphor.

Cobblers

Cobblers, usually preceded by 'a load of (old)' is

used to mean nonsense, rubbish or idiocy. It originated in cockney rhyming slang and, like most cockney rhymes, the logic behind it is odd, yet simple. In yesteryear, a cobbler's prize piece of kit was his awl, a tool that made neat holes in leather without which a cobbler was unable to cobble. Cobbler's awls was rhymed with balls. So, instead of calling something a load of balls, it was a load of cobblers. The word old was simply thrown in as an intensifier. Whether the link with awls was merely one of convenient rhyme, or whether the fact that awls, like balls, were essential, precious things, it is hard to say, but it all fits together too nicely to be a coincidence – or maybe the comparison is just a load of old cobblers.

Dead as a doornail

We may remark that a plant, animal, person or perhaps even a relationship is as dead as a doornail in order to emphasise that the object we speak of is well and truly finished. The term dates back to the fourteenth century and is borrowed from the technical jargon of carpentry. Clinching is a technique where a nail is hammered through a piece of wood and, once through, its end is bent so it is flat against the wood and cannot be pulled out again. Bending a nail of course renders it useless, which is why nails in this state were (and still are) referred to as dead. The phrase dead as a doornail came about as a simile because clinching was commonly practised in door-making. The short, tidy rhythm of the phrase created by the consonance of the two letters d might help to explain why it has stuck in an age of nail-free doors, while other 'dead as' phrases have themselves died and been forgotten.

Fits to a T

If something fits to a T, it is perfect for its purpose. The phrase is traditionally held to allude to a T square, used to measure a right angle precisely.

Fly off the handle

Picture the scene. You're not really the physical type and prefer the fulfilment of a good novel at the weekends rather than pottering about outside. However, someone in your household has impressed upon you the urgent need to chop firewood for the winter. Welcoming the chance to prove your masculine credentials, you take down the seldom-used axe you bought many seasons ago. You swing it back with gusto only to find that the wood that holds the head has shrunk and that the blade is now arching towards your kitchen window. When someone flies off the handle, they are behaving like an axe (or hammer) head that has come off its handle, threatening their surroundings with unselective destruction.

Hammer and tongs

To go at something (or conceivably someone) hammer and tongs is to put a large amount of effort into it (or them!). The expression derives from the profession of the blacksmith, who would use these instruments in his metal work. Involving as it did extreme heat, iron and muscle power, getting the desired results in the forge was no mean feat for a smith, so it is easy to see how this formed the basis of this 300-year-old phrase describing hard, dedicated work.

Make ends meet

To make ends meet is to ensure that one's income is sufficient to cover one's living costs. It often has slightly negative connotations, as it implies having no surplus income and that, rather than being in a position of wealth, a person who is making ends meet is merely living in an acceptable level of poverty. 'I'm only earning enough to make ends meet, nothing more,' the first-time jobber, fresh out of university, may lament on finding themselves in a big city on a small salary. The phrase dates from at least the seventeenth century, and finds its origins in bookkeeping. The end of the income column on a bookkeeper's ledger contains a figure, and for the books to balance this must match or exceed the corresponding figure at the bottom of the expenditure column. We can easily appreciate how the language of accounting transferred into that of everyday life.

CHAPTER SEVENTEEN:
AND FINALLY…

Best Man

AND FINALLY...

Beck and call

To be at someone's beck and call is to be on standby to do their bidding. It is a phrase that comes from the world of the days when everyone from the middle classes up could afford a servant. The beck part of the phrase is a shorter version of the word beckon. Beckoning is a discreet way of attracting a person's attention, a way of getting someone to do something without having to get involved with the bothersome business of actually speaking to them. Call, in this instance, means what it always does.

233

Best man

Best men by definition must be bold, courageous and intrepid. Nowadays they must fearlessly face a drunken assembly of two families who may feel uneasy in each other's company, if not hostile. It is their duty not to lose the bride's wedding ring – a small, expensive piece of jewellery. Men are not generally good at looking after that kind of thing. They must also keep the groom sober and upstanding, which may be impossible. The trials the original 'best men' faced were even greater. In the fourth or fifth century in Northern Europe, legend has it that a groom would take his strongest and most trusted friend with him to abduct a woman of his choice and marry her. The fact that whoever was chosen for the task was always the best man for the job led to the role of best man being created. One of the best man's duties would be to beat back angry relatives as they burst in on the ceremony. This is also alleged to be the reason why the bride stands on the left of the groom and best man: if things got nasty, they could draw their swords (with their right hands) and defend the bride.

Bloke

Today, bloke is generally used in the UK as a casual term for 'man'. Interestingly, though, it is not an exclusively British word – Americans have used it for 200 years to mean 'stupid idiot'. The word is Romany in origin.

Boxing Day

One would be hard-pressed to find a soul in England who does not know that Boxing Day is the day after Christmas Day, although most of us don't have a clue as to why the day is so named. Well, it certainly has nothing to do with the sport. In seventeenth-century Britain, it was common at Christmas for apprentices to carry around ceramic boxes, named Christmas boxes, in case their masters' customers were kind enough to offer seasonal gifts of money. The money was then to be shared among everyone in the company as an end-of-year bonus. A century on, the term Christmas box had lost its specific meaning and had come to represent any financial gift bequeathed by a member of the public to tradesmen, postmen, policemen and the like to thank them and wish them season's greetings. Over the next 100 years it became more and more of a custom for public-service employees (and, increasingly, anyone who felt like asking!) to request financial donations by knocking on doors or merely approaching people on the street the day after Christmas Day. Presumably the logic behind requesting gifts on this day was that, of all days in the year, the day after Christmas (when so much giving had been done) there would be plenty of people laden with unwanted gifts, or with guilt about their good fortunes, who would be only too pleased to be unburdened of either. Hence, in the eighteenth century, the day became known as Boxing Day.

Brownie points

You can earn brownie points in Brownies (the junior version of Girl Guides); however, debate rages as to whether that's quite the same thing as the brownie points you earn by sucking up to someone. Stateside, brownie points in the 1950s were very specifically negative: they may have ingratiated you with an authority figure, but they isolated you from decent people. Why then, if they are not related to the Brownies, are they brown? Delicately put, the phrase shares its imagery with *Private Eye*'s Order of the Brown Nose and the phrase to 'brown nose' someone.

Cack-handed

If we label somebody cack-handed, we are most likely lambasting them for an act of clumsiness or inept management of a situation. Many of us will be familiar with 'cack' as a word for faeces, yet few would link this meaning with the phrase. Excrement is, however, vital to the term's origin, for the old English word *cack* is linked to the ancient tradition of wiping oneself in the toilet with the left hand, saving the right for more salubrious and dignified acts. To wipe oneself with the right hand would therefore have been to do it the wrong way around. Left-handed people were seen as people who did everything the wrong way around, and who generally looked rather clumsy. In the nineteenth century such folk were given this unfortunate label, and over time anyone who performed any act incorrectly was seen as such, whether left-handed or not.

Chinless wonder

This is an insult aimed squarely at the British upper classes. In this conceit, the inbreeding thought to plague the higher echelons of British society has, through time, resulted in not only the diminishing of the noble brain, but also the stately chin. The use of the word wonder is, of course, ironic.

Clutching at straws

If we are clutching at straws, we are more often than not making a desperate attempt to save ourselves from losing an argument, or from falling foul of a situation. The attempt is unlikely to be effective, and the phrase comes from the proverb 'A drowning man will clutch at straws'. First found in the work of Thomas More (1478–1535), the proverb has taken various forms since, but its meaning has never varied.

Crackpot

A crackpot is a person whose mental faculties are not quite intact – he or she is a bit of a nutter, and may be wont to come up with crackpot schemes. Originally, in the late nineteenth century, crackpot referred merely to an idiotic or dim person. The words compares the mind contained within a head with a pot ('pot' having then been slang for head). A cracked pot is, of course, not fully functional. The modern sense of crackpot referring to someone filled with peculiar notions, mad ideas or afflicted with downright lunacy, developed in the early twentieth century.

Dab hand

Somebody who is particularly skilful at a particular job. You might hear someone say, 'He's a dab hand at fixing furniture,' indicating that the person has a certain *je ne sais quoi* when it comes to carpentry. There are two theories surrounding how 'dab' in this context came to mean what it does. Although it sounds like a slang word, it could be a corruption of 'adept'. There is also evidence that the word might simply be an extended use of 'dab' in the sense of to lightly touch, similar to the way we might carefully dab at a stain with a wet cloth.

Fast as quicksilver

The common name for the metal mercury was once quicksilver. Mercury itself is very shiny, explaining the comparison with silver. 'Quick' in this instance meant 'alive', and the reason for this description is that mercury is the only commonly occurring metal that is a liquid at room temperature. When poured on to a surface, it often appears to 'run away' in droplets.

Give it some welly

This is a phrase dating from the late 1960s, often used to encourage someone to try a little harder at what they are doing. Often preceded by 'Go on!', the expression is frequently employed as a criticism of a person's lack of effort, but also works as a comment designed to bolster the resolve of someone who is already hard at it. The phrase is linked to wellington boots (protective waterproof footwear named after the First Duke of Wellington). In a slightly quirky, abstract sort of way, wellies here are associated with the use of the foot to boot or kick with effort – the idea seems to be that to engage in kicking (or indeed any sort of vigorous exercise involving the lower body!) while sporting a pair of wellies would require considerably more effort than the same activity performed in normal footwear. A wonderfully quirky piece of British slang.

Grotty

Grotty is a truncation of 'grotesque'. Grotesque is a word that has become strangely distorted in meaning through the centuries. Originally it described a style of painting found in the grottos – or crypts – of medieval Italian churches. The figures in the paintings were often unnaturally distorted. Now grotesque may well mean bizarre, but it has an added sense of ugliness and unpleasantness. As a word, grotty goes straight for the unpleasant aspects of the grotesque and also has an added filthy, squalid edge.

Having one's guts for garters

Having one's guts for garters, a term so beloved of schoolteachers, managers, parents and just about anyone in a position of authority, is a phrase whose imagery we rarely stop to consider. When examined, the phrase conjures a grotesque act and, while it has always been used figuratively, it was originally a grave warning used to give a threat of real violence. Originating in the early 1800s, it began life in east London as cockney slang and weathered the years until it became an oft-used warning between ranks in the Second World War. We still use the phrase today, but with a degree of light-heartedness, to indicate that a punishment of sorts will be meted out to an unfortunate subordinate who has taken the wrong action in a situation.

How's your father

This is a question we might legitimately ask anyone in touch with their paternal figure, but it also has a comic function as a daft and cheeky slang euphemism for casual sex. Normally incorporated into a question along the lines of "'Ello, love, how about a bit of how's your father?', it is a seriously outmoded English expression and, these days, would only be used as an ironic reference to a bygone era of political incorrectness and *Carry On* film humour. The phrase was made popular by Harry Tate, a turn of the century music-hall entertainer who crafted his shows so that, when seemingly tongue-tied or unable to answer a question, he would change the subject by asking, 'How's your father?' Early twentieth-century audiences found this hilarious, and it became a catchphrase used to stand in for anything the speaker chose – Harry Tate used it as a substitute for an answer, others used it as a substitute for more risqué propositions. The latter usage caught on and still elicits a giggle to this day!

Hurly-burly
Hurly-burly is defined in the *Oxford English Dictionary* as 'boisterous activity; commotion', and it is a shortened version of the much older phrase hurling and burling. Here, the word hurling is used in an old sense of rough behaviour and commotion. Burling is not a word in itself, but rather just a rhyming variation used to create a pleasant-sounding euphony.

Kick the bucket

To die. There are competing theories here and, fittingly for a phrase describing death, neither is especially nice. The first one refers to suicide. The depressed person stands on a bucket, the noose tight about their neck, and kicks the bucket from beneath themselves. The second describes the practice of slaughtering a pig by hanging it from a beam, an old word for which is 'bucket'. As the pig died, it would kick against the beam.

Laser

Laser has become such a commonly used word it is often forgotten that it is an acronym: Light Amplification by the Stimulated Emission of Radiation. The American Gordon Gould invented the first optical laser in 1958, but didn't apply for a patent until the following year, which some feel has left his claim to be its inventor in doubt. He was certainly the first to use the word laser, and most people acknowledge him as the laser's creator.

Mollycoddle

Moddycoddling is the act of fussing over somebody and pandering to their needs in a fussy and indulgent way. Mollycoddlers are nearly always women. Molly is a familiar form of Mary, and in the 1700s it was used pejoratively to refer to gay men, who were called Miss Mollies. So there is a strong association with femininity here, as there is in the meaning of coddle – to be protective of somebody and to act accordingly. Interestingly, coddle derives from caudle, a drink given to the ill. These senses of protectiveness and looking after the ill combine to produce today's meaning of the word. As a noun, mollycoddle traditionally meant (and still occasionally does mean) a particularly effeminate man. The verb grew out of this in the 1800s and, even though modern usage does not always refer to homosexuality, there are sometimes unpleasant homophobic and sexist undertones when one person accuses another of being mollycoddled and therefore slightly effeminate.

Nip in the bud

A gardening expression that means to stop something in its early stages. The bud in discussion is that from which a flower grows. As any gardener knows, it's not always good to have plants growing in all directions, or even flowering. Sometimes you would rather the plant grew in other directions, or saved the energy it would have expended in producing flowers.

Quack

The word quack wasn't always applied to ducks. It's an old Dutch word that describes someone who chatters and babbles. Around the sixteenth century, a term quacksalver came into use in England: it described medicine men who would hawk their dubious potions most vocally about the towns. The 'salver' part of the word means 'salve', which even today still retains some meaning as an ointment-type substance. Quacksalver was soon shortened to quack and, because of its association with curing ailments, started being used to describe bogus doctors.

Right as rain

Right as rain is one of those phrases we all use to emphasise that someone or something is very well, or just right, yet we probably have not stopped to try and make sense of the expression. After all, we may well question the reason behind comparing something being right with drops of water plummeting from the sky and drenching us. Indeed, rain is often something we complain about, and it rarely seems to come along at the right moment! So why the comparison? There is no definitive answer, but if we consider that rain is considered to fall in a straight line, and then reflect that 'straight' can denote truthfulness and honesty, the comparison doesn't seem so strange. Also, despite the fact of rain being an annoyance, it is paradoxically something we all depend on. Combine this with an age-old association of water with purity (and therefore truth), the association of rainwater with something that is right makes sense. The alliteration sounds good too, which may explain why the phrase has been in use for just over a century.

Snake-oil merchant

A snake-oil merchant is someone who tries to sell you a load of old rubbish. Snake oil is a too-good-to-be-true elixir from somewhere you've never heard of, which will make you attractive to the opposite sex, give you a full head of hair, cure the incurable and generally do the impossible. Such salesmen were especially prevalent in the United States in the nineteenth century, although you can go pretty much anywhere to find this kind of thing. It is unlikely that these men dealt exclusively in snake oil, but the use of strange animal products goes hand in hand with the idea of weird and wonderful magical potions that sound better than they actually are.

Software

Software refers to computer programs, as opposed to the equipment on which software is operated – hardware. Hardware, of course, is not exclusively associated with computers, being used to describe ironmongery, pots, pans, kettles – and it is still used in the military parlance for guns 'n' ammo. The point is that software doesn't change the essential elements of the hardware. It is changeable and movable.

Spend a penny

'I'm going to spend a penny' is a very nice way of saying that you're about to pay a trip to the lavatory. It became popular in the 1940s when the price of admission to a public loo was a penny.

Spitting image

To be the spitting image of someone is to bear a very close resemblance to them. The word spit in this phrase is used figuratively to suggest that two people are so similar in appearance that one could have been spat out by the other. Originally it was spit 'n' image, then spit and image, relating to the idea of spitting and producing an identical image.

Third degree

If we are given the third degree, we are intensively questioned on a subject by a suspicious, or perhaps merely interested, party until the subject is exhausted. The term comes directly from the Freemasons. The top-ranking

Masons are called Third Degree Masons, and in order to gain this title a member must undergo severe and thorough scrutiny and questioning from superiors until they are satisfied of his trustworthiness.

Tip

When leaving a tip for a waiter, many people believe they are leaving something whose origin lies in the acronym of To Improve Performance. They are mistaken. Its true origin is far more exciting. Tip is a thirteenth-century word meaning to touch lightly. The word developed over the next 400 years until, in the 1600s, it became synonymous with giving something to another person with a degree of slyness or craftiness. The original sense of touching lightly is still present in this meaning – to pass something to another while escaping notice requires a light, barely discernible touch. It was not until the eighteenth century that the modern sense of giving an extra financial acknowledgement of good service developed. Still, though, the idea of touching lightly, and being discreet, is present in our use of the word.

Turn over a new leaf

Leaf is a semi-archaic term for a page. To turn over a new leaf, therefore, is to turn to a new page in a book. In this phrase the book is most likely to be a journal or diary, where the new blank page gives you a fresh chance to fulfil your good intentions.

Willy-nilly

In our times, the phrase willy-nilly means disorganised and haphazard. We can carry out a task in a willy-nilly way, without plans or a sense of order. When used in speech, the speaker is often criticising someone ('Well, if you think you can just apply for any old job willy-nilly and get it, you've got another think coming!'). Its use originates from the seventeenth century, when the phrase will I, nill I was used in a different sense, that of the need for a task to be completed whether or not one wishes to undertake it or not (will means one's desire to do, and nill means the opposite – one's desire not to do). Someone who is obligated to do something, but who may or may not be willing to do it may well end up performing the task in a rather ill-thought-through manner, resulting in a sloppy, incomplete job. Will I, nill I became a term for such situations. It turned into willy-nilly, and in doing so its meaning expanded into the modern sense.

Yonks

'It's been yonks,' we often say, in all probability speaking of something that has not been done or to someone we have not seen for a long period of time. There is no definitive explanation of this word's origin, but the most often cited and most sensible offering says that the term is a shortened and rearranged form of donkey's years.

INDEX TO PHRASES